PENGUIN BOOKS

BBC BOOKS

ONE AND TWO HALVES TO K2

Yorkshireman James Ballard, 49, sometime designer, engineer and photographer, lived with climber Alison Hargreaves for fifteen years in Derbyshire, Scotland and France. They were married in 1988. He has travelled and climbed extensively in Europe and America, as well as journeying to Everest base camp with Alison and their two children in 1994. Jim lives in the shadow of Ben Nevis in the Scottish Highlands and devotes himself to bringing up Tom and Kate, mountain adventures, climbing, skiing, mountain biking, writing and photography.

D1483851

ONE AND TWO HALVES TO K2

JAMES BALLARD

PENGUIN BOOKS
BBC BOOKS

PENGUIN BOOKS
BBC BOOKS

Published by the Penguin Group and BBC Worldwide Ltd
Penguin Books Ltd, 27 Wrights Lane, London W8 5TZ, England
Penguin Books USA Inc., 375 Hudson Street, New York, New York 10014, USA
Penguin Books Australia Ltd, Ringwood, Victoria, Australia
Penguin Books Canada Ltd, 10 Alcorn Avenue, Toronto, Ontario, Canada M4V 3B2
Penguin Books (NZ) Ltd, 182–190 Wairau Road, Auckland 10, New Zealand

Penguin Books Ltd, Registered Offices: Harmondsworth, Middlesex, England

First published by BBC Books, an imprint of BBC Worldwide Publishing, 1996
Published in Penguin Books 1996
1 3 5 7 9 10 8 6 4 2

This book was first published to accompany the television programme *Inside Story:
Alison's Last Mountain*, which was broadcast in February 1996. The programme was
produced by BBC Television Documentaries Department.
Series Editor: Olivia Lichtenstein
Producers: Roger Courtiour and Christopher Terrill
Director: Christopher Terrill

THIS BOOK IS DEDICATED TO THE PEOPLE OF PAKISTAN
WHOSE SUPPORT, CARE AND AFFECTION WAS EVER-PRESENT
THROUGHOUT THE ENTIRE ADVENTURE.

Mother of mountains
Such wonders you conceive
How can one so small
Dream of measuring their scale?

RAJA CHANGEZ SULTAN
FROM *THE HIMALAYAN ODYSSEY*

ACKNOWLEDGEMENTS

The adventure that is at the centre of this book would have been impossible without the support of the friends who agreed to join me and my children on our journey to the Baltoro: Cath Collier, David Collier, Cally Fleming and Ian Sutherland. My heartfelt thanks also go to Roger Courtiour and Heather Holden-Brown for having faith in the adventure. To all the kind people, friends, acquaintances and strangers who have written letters of congratulation following Alison's success on Everest and condolence following her death on K2, my deepest thanks. The book itself only came into being because of the dedication and hard work of Laura Kibby, who turned my handwritten notes and tapes into acceptable English. The whole would be poorer without her.

CONTENTS

ALISON'S MAP FOR TOM AND KATE SENT

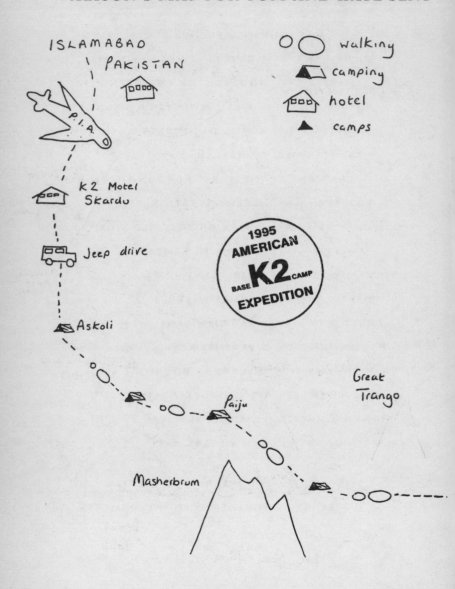

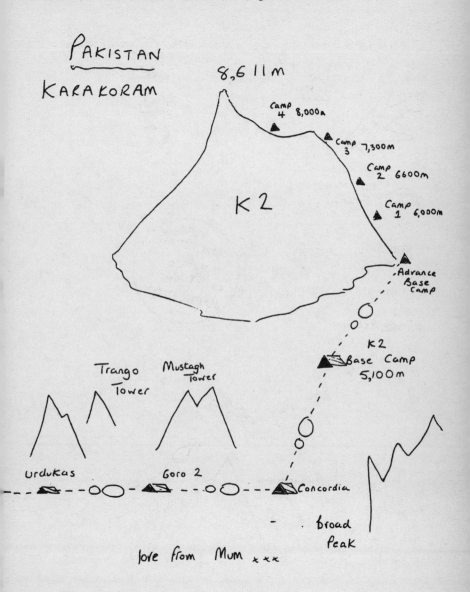

CHAPTER ONE

MUM'S LAST MOUNTAIN

*'It is better to live for one day as a tiger
than for a thousand years as a sheep'*

TIBETAN PROVERB

The telephone rang. I picked it up, my mind still in the detective novel I was reading. Tom, six, and Kate, four, had just gone off to sleep and I did not want to wake them. The soft, tobacco-hoarse voice at the end of the line was instantly recognizable as that of Joe Quinn, the Press Association's bureau chief in Scotland. He was hesitant and apologetic.

'Mr Ballard, er Jim. I don't know how to start this, but have you heard from America that a story about your wife on K2 has been put out on the Internet?'

I caught my breath. 'Go on.' Quickly, he read through the communiqué, pausing to let me take it in.

'Alison Hargreaves, 33, Scottish mountaineer and a rising star in the international climbing community, was killed Sunday 13 August 1995 shortly after reaching the summit of Pakistan's K2.'

Joe's voice trailed away. The hairs on the back of my neck stood up. I grappled desperately to make sense of the information that had just washed over me. Something deep inside told me it was true. Alison was dead.

Almost immediately a car's headlights shot over the brow of the hill in front of our Highland cottage nestling in Scotland's Great Glen. The vehicle pulled to a stop outside. As I opened the door Alison Hood, a friend from the Nevis Range ski resort where Alison was a mountain advisor, staggered into my arms clutching a fax. 'I am so, so sorry Jim,' she choked, tears rolling down her face. We held each other for a few moments. I tried, vainly, to tell myself that it could just be an error or a case of mistaken identity. I needed to know more, right away. Back inside, I got on the phone to the States and began dialling all the numbers I knew until I managed to track down Michael Kennedy, the respected editor of America's *Climbing* magazine. He had climbed with Alison in Chamonix, France, and Alison had taken his wife Julie on her first major alpine ascent. The pain and anguish in his voice said it all. We went through the fax together.

Six other climbers in two separate groups also died Sunday: New Zealander Bruce Grant, Canadian Jeff Lakes and American Rob Slater, who had been climbing with Hargreaves; as well as three unidentified members of a five-person Spanish team. New Zealander Peter Hillary, son of Everest pioneer Sir Edmund Hillary and a member of the Hargreaves group, turned back early during the fateful summit bid and survived. Details of the accident remain sketchy but, according to Scott Fischer, a Seattle-based climber who was leading an expedition up nearby Broad Peak, the victims appear to have succumbed to a combination of bitter cold and 'brutal, brutal wind, 100 mph plus' during a sudden mountain storm. Fischer, who spoke via a satellite phone from base camp on the Baltoro glacier, said that spotters watching the climbers from a lower camp reported seeing at least one unidentified mountaineer fall. Kevin Cooney, a Colorado climber who arrived with Hargreaves at K2 base camp on 25 June but had to leave on 6 August, said several earlier summit bids had been turned back by fierce mountain storms. 'The weather has been very uncooperative all summer,' Cooney said in an interview from Colorado. 'Every time we started to go high on the mountains, a snowstorm would force us back down'.

Alison's group had set off on Sunday morning from camp four up the notorious Abruzzi ridge. At 6.17 p.m. the base camp received a radio call indicating that Alison, Rob Slater and Bruce Grant had reached the summit. They were not heard from again. Like me, Michael felt there were too many facts coming out and too many coincidences for it not to be true. He rang off, promising to let me know as soon as he heard more. I tried to cling to the slimmest of hopes that Alison was still fighting her way down; if anyone could come out of this alive, she could. Each new report coming in was to make that more and more unlikely. Alison had been blown off the Abruzzi ridge above 8000 metres (26 247 feet). No-one could survive that. The 'Killer Mountain' had once again lived up to its name.

Yet the news wasn't sinking in. How could Alison be dead? Alison, so self-assured, always so vitally alive? Her last letter was still on my desk and I rummaged among the papers and correspondence until I found the cream sheet with its neat square handwriting. It was addressed 'K2 base camp' and dated Saturday 22 July. Today was Wednesday 16 August; I had received it a few days ago. I pictured her scribbling away in the glow from her head torch, tucked up in her sleeping bag, the pen clutched between icy fingers, all her thoughts with Tom and Kate. She had always written at night, even in the long drawn-out darkness of the Himalayas. If it wasn't a letter it would be her diary, which I had seen her fill out faithfully since I had first known her as a teenager.

'I will be here for another two weeks but on 6 August want to start to trek back to get the aeroplane on 13 August. I don't think I can face any longer here than that,' she had written miserably on the brief single sheet. To Tom and Kate she added, 'I am very fit and well, but missing very much not being at my own home. I will only be happy when I see you two terrors again.'

I thought back to 13 August, the day she died. What was she still doing on K2 when she should have been relaxing safe and warm on her flight home? Everything about the letter shouted that she was keen to leave the icy slopes of this hostile mountain as soon as possible. She had a flight from Islamabad arranged and her Balti porters booked. It was not until some days later that I learned from

Tyneside mountaineer Alan Hinkes, who had been part of the same American expedition led by Rob Slater, that Alison had decided to stay and give it 'one more go'. She had talked incessantly about the children, he said, but in his opinion had become obsessed with reaching the summit.

Our lives had been turned upside down since Alison's return from Everest's lofty summit in May 1995, the first woman to reach the 8848-metre (29 029-feet) peak without oxygen and completely unsupported. How pleased she had been that her clothing sponsor Spraywray had produced a T-shirt to honour her climb bearing the slogan 'No oxygen, no sherpas, no equal'. The photograph she took during her special forty-five minutes on the summit sat on the mantelpiece. There she was on the world's highest mountain, smiling from underneath layer upon layer of warm fleece and insulation with only blue sky and snow behind her. It had been her greatest mountaineering achievement. Her first radio message down to base camp had been for her children. The climbers there heard her cry through the thin air and emptiness, 'I'm on top of the world and I love you dearly'.

Overnight she had become the media's new darling. They hounded her for interviews and personal appearances during her two weeks at home before she set off once more, this time for K2, the world's second highest mountain. Her ambition had been to complete the hat trick and climb Kanchenjunga next spring, becoming the first woman to reach the world's three highest peaks. The media used their column inches and airtime to alternately slate and praise her for combining motherhood with her choice of life-risking profession. For Alison there was no dilemma. When she was at home with the children she gave them her undivided attention, but when she was on a mountain her maternal feelings had to be put on hold: there was no time to think of anything but the job in hand. She had always wanted a family and when Tom and Kate came along she was delighted, but she had no intention of giving up her great passion for the mountains. She climbed the north face of the Eiger when she was six months pregnant with Tom and had been climbing on the day he was born.

To Tom and Kate, mountaineering was what Mum did and they never questioned it. It was only in the media that she had to justify her chosen occupation. In her last interview, which she gave to Matt Comeskey at K2 base camp (reproduced in the *Independent* on 2 September 1995), she tried to describe why she needed both. 'My kids are pretty active, they need a lot of time and energy, which is great. But sometimes you need a break...When you're with kids they demand, demand, demand and there's no give, give, give. And of course solo climbing is totally self-indulgent. You do what you want to do.'

On another occasion she explained in a *Sunday Telegraph* interview (27 November 1994), 'So much of climbing has to come from the head. You can't afford to stop and wonder how the kids are. That could be very distracting, that breaks your concentration and causes problems...Alison the Climber has to be self-sufficient and fully focused, with no-one to answer to or call upon – separate from Alison the Mother.'

A joint decision meant we devoted ourselves full-time to Alison's professional climbing career from 1992. The following year she had her first big break when she successfully soloed the six classic north faces of the Alps. It was an awesome achievement. We had spent the summer camping and living out of Perkins, our battered old Land-Rover, and as Alison climbed, I looked after the children and found myself enjoying it. Each night on their mother's return I would cook up a huge bowl of pasta and we would sit around listening to her adventures. We worked to the same formula when Alison made her first, this time unsuccessful, attempt on Everest in the autumn of 1994 when Tom, Kate and I accompanied her to base camp. By the time Alison returned to Everest in the spring, Tom had started school in Scotland. We felt it would be unfair to uproot him, so I resumed my 'new man' role and stayed in the Highlands to look after the children.

Upon her return from Everest, Alison had desperately wanted some time alone with Tom and Kate and promised them that K2 would be her last mountain until the following spring. A friend, Cally Fleming, lent her their family's caravan, which was hidden away on a delightfully remote spot near Oban, allowing Alison to escape for a magical few days by the seaside with Tom and Kate. It was a precious holiday for her. Little did anyone realize quite how special those few snatched moments would be. Tom still talks about the days on the beach collecting shells with his mum and climbing the small mountains behind.

Alison's departure day had been crazily rushed. We had moved into our first real home in three years. Alison had chosen the house and wanted to see the family settled in before she left. We packed our few belongings from the wooden chalet at nearby Spean Bridge, which had been our temporary base, into Perkins II, a Volkswagen camper that had replaced Perkins I. Alison offered to drive so I decided to make the most of my last morning of freedom before taking over sole responsibility for Tom and Kate. I cycled over to meet them at Nevis Range.

My lungs rasped as I pounded the pedals to the ridge of the forest track. Below me the undulating forest of Norwegian spruce and larch rolled down to the ski centre. I could see Alison, Tom and Kate, hijacked by yet another film crew. The high-summer smell of sweet gorse and heather was exhilarating. I did not hurry. When I finally reached them Tom was bursting with energy and decided he wanted to cycle to the cottage with me. We set off, leaving Kate and Alison to follow later in the camper. Tom complained about the cold so I draped my huge fleece jacket over his tiny body. Speeding tourists shot past us on the busy Fort William to Inverness road. I felt myself age by the minute as I watched my six-year-old zip along in front of me, oblivious to the dangers of the vehicles passing within inches of his painfully exposed body. It seemed an eternity before we were finally able to slip off on to the private estate track, rattle across a cattle grid and merge back into the wilderness.

The noise of traffic became no more than a distant rumble, until even that was replaced by the chomping of the grazing sheep, our new neighbours. Surrounded by fields and tucked away down a small incline, Stone Cottage was barely visible until we were right in front of it. The two-storey house stood alone in Scotland's Great Glen and fronted most of the Nevis range of mountains, the black-browed north face of Ben Nevis towering monstrously above us. Closer in, the serpentine ridge of Carn Beag Dearg to Carn Mor Dearg snaked menacingly in the shadows, while Aonach Mor, with its line of gondola ski lifts, was in the foreground, a lush carpet of pines rising up to meet it.

Visiting his new home for the first time, Tom jumped off his bike in excitement. It clattered on its side, wheels still spinning, as we unlocked the big oak door and let ourselves in. We had a quick look round, impressed by its spacious rooms and fantastic views. It was an ideal spot to drink in the splendour. Just as we started to move boxes into the right rooms our peace was shattered by two bundles of energy that spilled into the polished stone-tiled hall. Kate and Alison had arrived. Tom and I went to meet them and, with a look that I have known for so many years, Alison asked only with her eyes for approval. At last we were all there. I smiled. Alison could tell we felt at home and her face beamed.

That day, Saturday 10 June, was the last time our small family was to see Alison. We dropped her off at the Nevis Range office door where she was to do a television interview, then head down to London to review the Sunday papers on *Breakfast with Frost* before her flight to Pakistan and the long trek to K2 base camp. Alison had been torn over whether to accept as it meant sacrificing one more treasured day with the children, but she recognized it was too good an opportunity to pass up.

I remember how Alison had looked smaller even than her 5 feet 2 inches as she folded her arms around Tom and Kate and whispered, 'Be good for Daddy. Have lots of adventures to tell me about when I come home.' She looked up at me. We did not touch. We never did when it was time to part. 'Have a good time lass, take care of yourself and come back safely,' was all I could say. Alison turned her face away but not before I saw it distort with emotion as the tears welled up inside her. Tom and Kate clung to her as they always did when it was time to leave. I climbed back inside the car, putting the children in the back, and drove away. In the mirror I watched her wave, her face once more wearing a relaxed smile.

Both of us were climbers; we knew the risks involved but they were never discussed. Alison's own philosophy was, 'You never get a second chance but I love life so my aim is always to minimize the risks.' I remember how it had shocked her when, on one of her solo ascents in the Alps, she came across the clothes, equipment and contorted body of a fallen Spanish climber. She said later, 'It never crossed my mind that it could have been me. You can't think like that.' We both knew K2's reputation and its enormous death toll – it had already claimed thirty-eight lives. But her thoughts were on the possibility of summit success, not on the worst scenario. As for me, I never dwelt on thoughts of death. If you climb, you accept the risks, it's as simple as that. A climbing death is not a tragedy.

The harsh ring of the telephone brought me back with a start. The Internet message was being picked up all over the world and calls were coming in thick and fast. I tried to reach Cally, who also headed Alison's management company, set up to deal with the sponsorship, writing and lecturing fees that financed our unorthodox lifestyle. I was told she was out mountain biking but would be back soon.

Meanwhile, it was time to tell Alison's family: her parents, John and Joyce, older sister Sue and younger brother, Richard. For ten years I had tried to prepare myself for this day, ever since Alison had first visited the Himalayas for hard alpine climbs – in 1985, Alison, along with Jeff Lowe, Tom Frost and Mart Twight, completed the first ascent of a new route on Kantega, 6779 metres (22 235 feet). Knowing it was always a possibility did not make the job any less painful. The carefully rehearsed lines were forgotten. Down the phone line, as I broke the news, all I could sense was shock. I replaced the receiver. The phone rang again straight away. It was Cally. I told her what I knew. The silence hurt. 'Fuck, fuck, fuck, fuck, Jim...what should we do, should I come over to the house?' I was still numb. I hadn't thought about what to do.

'Yes, you had better come over so we can sort out the details,' I replied quietly. Alison regarded her professionalism highly. I had helped with her PR throughout her career; I could not let her down now.

Cally's partner John Wrighton drove her over from their home near Ballachulish, 20 miles away. Tom must have known intuitively something was wrong, for no sooner had they arrived than I heard his little feet stumbling down the wooden staircase. A few minutes later I picked up the soft whimper of Kate's night-time cry. John offered to get them back to sleep so that Cally, Alison Hood (who we knew as 'Hooders') and I could work out a strategy to deal with the news. We talked but I could not concentrate and eventually gave up. Cally and Hooders went up to beds in the spare room and told me to get some sleep. It was already Thursday. John offered me a cigarette, which I accepted, even though I had not smoked for years. He lit it, then, handing me the rest of the packet, shook my hand and climbed into his van. He had an early start with the Nevis Range hill crew the next morning.

I climbed into my big empty bed. The novel that had gripped me previously held nothing but blurred words as my mind whirled off in a kaleidoscope of images. Fifteen years together out of her thirty-three was a long time, almost a lifetime. Sleep would not come. The house was quiet. I got dressed and slipped across the hall to my desk and switched on my word processor. With my basic keyboard technique I painstakingly tapped out a press release.

At 4.00 a.m. the pitter-patter of tiny feet sounded at the door again. This time it was Kate who, like Tom, was still unaware of the heartbreaking news. 'Daddy, I just wanted a hug.' A soft four-year-old was in my arms and asleep before she had finished the sentence. I slotted her into the far side of my bed still clutching her favourite red silk scarf and Kipper, her cuddly toy dog. Restless, I walked outside. The early morning light was just beginning to seep over the horizon and I could tell it was going to be yet another stunning summer's day. I sat down on the front step and pulled out one of John's cigarettes. The cheap plastic lighter rasped into life, flashed out a weak orange flame, and I inhaled heavily.

The familiar mountain view in front of me dissolved. My mind took me on a voyage to other mountains and better times. Memories that only meant something to me and mine…Kate, aged two, in a huge sleeping bag, propped up in a child's car seat, her face lit with the gentle reds and oranges of her and Tom's first camp fire when we were all alone in the picture-postcard setting of Ailefroide, high in the French Dauphin Alps…

…Spring 1993 and waking the children to see the sunrise over Mont Blanc. We were bivouacking at 3048 metres (10 000 feet) by the rocky shore of Lac Blanc. The Chamonix valley slept below. We enjoyed the finest vista the European Alps have to offer in absolute solitude. As Tom first, then Kate, struggled to sit up, the ice that formed on the outside skin of their Gortex bivvi bags cracked and sloughed off like a glass skin. That fascinated the children. The mountains may have been bathed in early morning light as the sun shimmered like fire on the horizon but they simply slipped back into the natural womb-like warmth of their huge adult-sized sleeping bags. Alison and I looked at each other. What could you say? Alison too was soon lulled back to her slumbers and only I continued to sit with bone-cold fingers trying to record the scene for posterity through my camera lens…

The cigarette in my hand had burned down unsmoked and was scorching my fingers. I let it fall and ground it into the tarmac with my boot. I fired up another but could not stop myself from sinking back into the comfort of memories. What should have been Aonach Mor became the sun burning off the pre-dawn mist from Pumori, one of Everest's sister mountains. I was looking at the view from my side of the family tent when we were in the Himalayas during Alison's first ill-fated attempt on Everest a year ago. Beside me Alison, Tom and Kate lay in a cosy row in their sleeping bags…

The mists of my mind swirled again…I was driving along the side of the river Derwent in Derbyshire on an ethereal October morning. I had just witnessed the birth of Tom. I smiled as I remembered the daft little things; how, when I got home, I had fallen asleep with my bowl of cornflakes in front of me, only to wake an hour later without having spilt a drop. A child was born. A birth; a death. The wheel of life. The mountains had needed Alison for themselves but her spirit would live on in all of us. I climbed into bed. This time I did sleep. The rise and fall of Kate's breathing was all I needed.

Barely two hours later it was time to face the world. I gave Tom and Kate their breakfast and we were soon joined by Hooders and Cally. Kate thought it was great having company as she tucked into her cereal. Tom was more subdued. I wondered if he sensed something. I was driven round to Nevis Range and struggled to hold on to my feelings as, one by one, members of the hill crew shook my hand with tears running down their weather-beaten faces. By 10.00 a.m. the car park was full of reporters, photographers and film crews. I watched them gather through the slatted blinds of the office. Half an hour later, locking all my turbulent emotions in some dark recess of my mind, I grabbed the press release from my desk and walked out into the bright sunshine.

Immediately the questions began as the cameras clicked and whirled. Did this assembled mass realize the short statement I read spoke for fifteen years, two children and all those rocky dangers and mountain summits? I felt the world needed to know. Alison had touched people's lives. With her achievement on Everest, and now on K2, with no help, no oxygen, just simple raw talent, the world had finally woken up to her climbing genius. A number of the reporters had been here for her greatest triumph, just a few months before. Her quiet dignity and resolve had affected them then. To many she had become a friend and they grieved for her in that way.

The photographer from the *Daily Express* lingered as the pack dispersed to their mobile phones and laptops. He gave me a cigarette. He wanted to talk. In January he had shot Alison on one of Aonach Mor's satellite peaks on a biting cold winter's day, the ground covered in ice and snow. I was also on the mountain a short distance away and you could see for ever, down to the sea lochs shimmering in the distance. When he had finished shooting, he had asked Alison to take some pictures of him to show his mates how cold it was. She told me afterwards how much she had enjoyed the role reversal.

Tom and Kate spent the day on the hills with friends while I faced the press. I found myself searching through the crowds in the Nevis Range car park for Tom's blond hair and Kate's strawberry-blonde curls long before they were due. They appeared with smiles on their faces and laughter in their eyes. They had been having fun. I knew I could not put off my responsibility any longer. I took their hands and we walked into the cool quiet of the Nevis Range boardroom. The blinds were drawn. We were on our own. No-one would disturb us. This was the absolute worst moment.

We sat on the floor, my back against a glass display case. I could feel the beat of Tom's and Kate's hearts. The granite face slipped and the real Jim Ballard surfaced, as can only happen with those you love. These two little people were part of me. I did not speak. They looked up, so innocent yet so aware something was wrong. The salt tears coursed gently down my face and dripped onto Kate's fleece-covered shoulders.

'Your mummy is lost in a mountain storm and I do not think you will ever see her again.' Nineteen words that summed up their lives.

They cried. Tom quietly. Kate put her arms around my neck and shouted. We hugged and for a few moments became one. The world had changed for them that instant on K2. Kate continued to sob. Tom looked up through tear-rimmed eyes.

'It's OK, Tom, you will always be able to speak to her. She will always be there in your head and her spirit will always be watching over you.' His intelligence shone through. He understood. How, I do not know, but in that instant I knew he realized the full implications of what I had said.

'Dad?'

'Yes, Tom?'

'Can we go and see Mum's last mountain?'

'Yes, we can and we will.'

'When?'

'In a few weeks. I will make you a promise and, as you know, Mum and I always kept our promises. We will go to K2, your mother's last mountain.'

CHAPTER TWO

NO PLACE FOR CHILDREN?

*'All men dream: but not equally. Those who dream by night in the
dusty recesses of their minds wake in the day to find that it was
vanity; but the dreamers of the day are dangerous men, for they may
act their dreams with open eyes, to make it possible.'*

T. E. LAWRENCE

Four weeks and a day later we stood at Fort William station ready to
board the night sleeper to London. Kate, determined to carry her
own small rucksack, dragged it along the platform, pushing away any
offers of help. It contained her small toy dog Kipper, Licky the lion
and a tiny teddy bear called Sherpani. Tom hung close to me with his
well-loved Brown Bear tucked under his arm. Brown Bear had been
everywhere with him and Tom was making sure that he was not going
to miss out on this trip. Our long journey to K2 was just beginning.

Neither Tom nor Kate appeared to have any worries about the
journey. To them this was a new adventure; once again they were
travelling to foreign parts and, as far as they were concerned, that
was always exciting. Behind us was a four-man BBC television crew
who were making a documentary of the trip, camera and sound
equipment perched on their shoulders filming our every move. All
were burly 6-footers whose well-built physiques would not have
looked out of place on a rugby pitch. I wondered if they had been
specially picked because of the demands of our journey.

The idea of visiting 'Mum's last mountain' had grown for Tom and
Kate in the days after I had broken the news that she was not coming
home. I noticed one of the postcards showing Alison on the summit
of Everest had appeared on Tom's bedside table. Kate seemed her

usual exuberant self but I could tell her young mind was searching
for answers. When I asked if she knew where we were going, she
would point to the shadows behind Ben Nevis. Tom, old enough to
remember the trip we had made as a family to Everest base camp in
1994, was more aware of the distances involved. The trek became a
focus for us all in the weeks that followed and I was glad to be able to
throw myself into organizing it.

Without any definite plan of action I had mentioned my promise
to Tom and our proposed trip to K2 to the assembled press pack
several weeks earlier. The reporters had lingered for days after news
of Alison's and the other six climbers' deaths first broke, their grey-
suited huddles in the Nevis Range forecourt so out of place in the
summer sunshine among the hill walkers and sightseers. Many of the
national titles had waded in, offering to underwrite the cost if they
could accompany me exclusively. One poor hack delegated to do
his newspaper's bidding admitted, through heavy puffs on his
cigarette, that he had never been out of Britain, even on a package
holiday. I sensed he would not be too disappointed if his paper lost
out on this one.

I did not want to profit in any way from Alison's death but my
priority was to take care of Tom and Kate; I was now a single parent
with two young children to support. I knew Alison's former sponsors
would help in any way they could and I was already being inundated
with assurances about the goodwill of the Pakistani Government.
That was when I was approached by the BBC, who wanted to
accompany us and make a documentary for *Inside Story*. I agreed to
meet one of their producers.

As I walked into the lobby of Fort William's Mercury Hotel a few
days later, Roger Courtiour rose from his seat to greet me. Slightly
built with a goatee beard and lived-in face, this was a man with a long
pedigree in journalism and documentary film-making. He ordered
tea and, as we chatted, I think we both realized we could work
together. I invited him back to the house to discuss the organizational
headaches involved. By the time he left, the trip only needed the

stamp of approval from the men in suits in London for planning to begin. We had shaken hands and, as far as I was concerned, that was it.

Details of Alison's last hours on K2 continued to trickle out. She had died after her third summit attempt. On one occasion, it was reported, she had become so frustrated by the bad weather that she flung down her rucksack and said she was off home to see her children. Something made her turn round and give it 'one last go'.

There were Peter Hillary's tales of the seven who died being gripped by 'summit fever'. He said a strange chemistry had built up between them that left them obsessed with getting there, no matter what. Together they had mistakenly believed there was safety in numbers, he reported. This did not sound like the Alison I knew; more like the language of a lurid adventure paperback. Only a year before she had pulled out just 400 metres (1312 feet) short of the summit of Everest on her first solo attempt because the cold had started to eat at her hands and feet. It was the thought of hugging Tom and Kate without fingers that persuaded her to make the heart-breaking decision to give up. Peter, who claimed he gave up his K2 summit bid that fateful Sunday because storms were closing in, said that 'it was a mistake for [the group] to go on the way they did'. But not only was Alison one of the greatest climbers in the world, she was also one of the most careful. She knew Tom and Kate were waiting for her at home. Would she be reckless? Never.

A different version of events emerged from the two surviving Spanish climbers, Lorenzo Ortas and Pepe Garcas. Their tents and equipment were blown away at camp four when the storms struck shortly after 7.00 p.m. on the night of 13 August. They were picked up by an army helicopter at base camp six days later, suffering from frostbite. Their interpretation of what happened was some way from Peter Hillary's. They described the weather as being perfect for climbing, even though it was very cold. Alison's decision to try for the summit did not appear to be the wrong one at the time. K2 is notorious for its changeable weather patterns: days of perfect weather can switch suddenly to horrendous storms as 100 mph-plus winds shoot across the Karakoram mountain range from China and Tibet. The Spaniards' only explanation was that a fierce wind must have blown up and taken Alison, swiftly and without suffering.

These two men brought me final confirmation of Alison's death. Any faint hope I had clung to that she was still alive ended with their reports that they had seen climbing equipment matching Alison's on the way down. A body they thought was hers was also spotted. I knew then that she would not be coming home.

It was becoming increasingly clear that the six other climbers had also perished. My thoughts went out to their families. Jeff Lakes was the only one of them I knew. Our association went back to Alison's first attempt on Everest in 1994, when Jeff had been attempting the adjacent Nepalese mountain of Lhotse, 8511 metres (27 923 feet) high. On that occasion, he and a fellow climber had been caught in a narrow gully high on the mountain by a ferocious storm. He radioed down because they thought they were going to die. Both were exhausted after being battered constantly by the winds and falling snow. Stuck on a half-hacked-out ice ledge, his partner was drifting into unconsciousness but Jeff had no intention of leaving him. He was determined they would both see it through or die in the attempt. On that occasion, by some miracle, they did escape.

Pencil-thin and ill, Jeff had caught up with us as we waited at Shyanboche, the airstrip that hangs on a hillside above the Sherpa capital Namche Bazaar. We were waiting for our helicopter to fly us out. We were heading back to Scotland and he to Australia. There was no room on the flight for him but, as the helicopter crew had already counted the numbers, I reasoned they would not bother to check again. If Jeff was to hold Tom's hand and Tom was to look up and talk to Jeff, no-one would think twice. He sat through the flight chatting to me and Tom and got back to Kathmandu squashed in the back of the ex-Russian Air Force chopper with the rest of us.

Jeff had been aiming for the K2 summit that fateful August Sunday but as Alison and the five others progressed up the Abruzzi ridge ahead of him he had changed his mind and instead headed down for camp four to wait for them to reach the top. The New Zealand/American camp on the shoulder of the ridge was struck by the storms as Jeff sheltered there. The camp was destroyed and he was badly savaged by the ferocious winds. Jeff escaped but faced a harrowing descent back down the mountain. It was made worse by the fact that camp three had been destroyed, so he had no choice but to continue downwards. He finally stumbled into camp two where he was found by Matt Comeskey, a New Zealander from his own expedition. Matt tried to push life back into Jeff's exhausted frame but during the night his spirit moved on. The battle against the elements had been too much for his worn-out body...

The last of our luggage was loaded into the guard's van at Fort William station. Tom, Kate and I were asked to assemble so the press pack could take some final departure shots. The usual questions were fired: 'Why are you making the trip?', 'When will you be back?' and so on. Then came the sting. 'Veteran mountaineer Doug Scott has said you should not be taking your children to K2. Is he right?' The same question had been fired at me over and over again in various guises over the previous four weeks. 'He has an opinion that I do not share, but he is of course entitled to it,' I replied through gritted teeth. I thought back to an interview Doug gave to his friend Greg Child for his book, *Mixed Emotions*, where he had talked about women climbers. 'I think women are up against it in alpine-style Himalayan climbing, mainly because they can't carry the same weight as men,' he had said, referring to the lightweight style of mountaineering where the climber carries his or her own load. 'They're certainly capable of Sherpa-assisted ascents but it would be a very exceptional pair of women who could climb one of the five highest 8000-metre summits totally alone.' I wondered where this left Alison's Everest climb. I have a lot of respect for dear old Doug but I felt his comments about taking the children were equally unfounded. He had taken his own children out to the Himalayas on his early trips and had enjoyed the pleasure of living with them at base camp many times. What had changed his attitude as the years rolled on?

Opposition to our trip to K2 had come first from Alison's mother and father. John and Joyce Hargreaves came up from Derbyshire to see Tom and Kate a few days after Alison's death. We weren't close and our relationship had usually been restricted to polite formalities but Alison's death changed that. The wind from the East that blew her from the mountain had rewritten all our lives. Although keen hill walkers themselves, mountaineering was not the career path they would have chosen for their daughter. When Alison and I met, I was thirty-four and running a climbing shop in Derbyshire; she was just eighteen and destined to follow in the family footsteps and read maths at Oxford. Alison, with a stubborn streak that I was to run into many times during our years together, was determined to plough her own furrow. She threw over academia for the mountains. The reason she gave later was that she had become passionate about climbing. 'I didn't feel I could handle going to Oxford. The idea of going down south away from the rocks was like...no way, you know?' she would say in interviews.

This passion began as a young girl, when she used to go hill walking with her family. It was a trip to Ben Nevis, aged about six, when she ran off in front of her parents to the top that confirmed for her the love of mountains that was to grow throughout her life. She was also encouraged to take up rock climbing by Hilary Collins, her school outdoor pursuits teacher (who later married Peter Boardman, the climber who disappeared on Everest's north-east ridge in 1982). Alison found it a great way to channel her aggression. She would tell me how, when she was fourteen, she went on a walking holiday to Austria and adored it so much there were tears pouring down her cheeks as she rolled up the blinds of her couchette on the train ride home and watched the Alps diminishing...

I had offered to pick up her parents from the local Spean Bridge station. They are very private individuals and although they joined me in front of the press they were clearly uncomfortable as the cameras snapped away. Then a reporter asked, 'What do you think about taking the children to K2?' They looked at each other, painfully conscious that I was nearby. 'We would rather they weren't going. It would be better if they went when they are a bit older,' John said awkwardly.

Their comments were pounced upon immediately and within days critics started to creep out of the woodwork. Suddenly, the world was full of experts who, the column inches and hours of airtime assured us, had spent all their mountaineering and outdoor lives shepherding children of all ages all over the world. Everyone seemed to have something to say. I was no longer capable of looking after my own children. I was panned for even contemplating taking them to this wild and lonely place. These were the people who had misunderstood Alison and her achievements. Alison's whole life had been about rebelling against the humdrum and expected; she was motivated by mountains and adventure. She certainly did not want her children to have to settle for anything less. I was obliged in Alison's spirit to make sure the children's lives remained the adventure she had wanted them to be. So far, their short lives had been packed with excitement but neither their mother nor I had ever been criticized before.

I wondered where all those so-called experts had been when Tom and Kate, aged four and two, had spent 180 nights camping high in the European Alps without so much as a sniffy nose between them. Ironically, the only time Tom had ever been ill was when he had a comfortable home in Derbyshire and attended the local school. He was afflicted by a continuous stream of colds and childish illnesses then.

Last winter, Kate and I had spent eighty days skiing in the Scottish mountains. When the weather prevented us from going on the pistes we just brought out the sledge. Sometimes the Arctic wind howling round the Nevis range was so wild that it shaped the snow into a series of jagged teeth across the normally smooth runs. Most of the skiers would leave but Kate and I simply donned our face masks, goggles and hard hats and carried on. I couldn't have dragged Kate away if I had tried. The faster the sledge went, the more we shot off the hard-packed peaks of snow. 'I want to go higher,' Kate would scream as we flew through the air with only space beneath us. Down we would smash through the powdery drifts in full flight, the wind whipping at our jackets, to come gliding in with a soft thump. On all the other days we would ski down the slopes together. Kate would jump up all smiles at the bottom and demand instantly, 'Let's go again'. We were usually the last off the hill when the worst of the weather finally closed in. No-one told me then they knew a better way for a young child to spend her time.

Even the Himalayas were not new territory for Tom and Kate. The children accompanied Alison and me to Nepal when she made her first attempt on Everest in 1994. For three months they thrived in conditions very similar to those we were now to face. Tom walked all the way to base camp and back, often leaving me puffing and panting far behind him. The image of him toddling happily away up the hills while every bone in my then forty-eight-year-old body told me I couldn't catch up with him is etched painfully in my memory. Kate spent most of the journey being carried on the back of Nima, a local girl from Lukhla referred to as a Sherpani, chatting merrily to everybody she passed. At Everest base camp, 5460 metres (18 000 feet) up on the Khumbu glacier, out would come the school books and Tom would study his lessons much as if he were in his centrally heated classroom back home. The same when it was bath-time: Alison would simply fill up a big aluminium bowl with steaming hot water, sit it on a barrel on the glacier and give them a good scrub. Tom and Kate just accepted this was the way of life.

I, more than anyone, do not want anything to happen to the two people who mean most to me in the world. Of course there are risks taking children to a third-world country but the experience gained is likely to be far more rewarding for them than being kept cosseted in cotton wool all their lives. K2 is remote; so remote that even the locals have failed to come up with a name that sticks, which is why it is still known by the original cartographer's number (although trendy Europeans with an ethnic bent have conjured up 'Chogri' or even 'Chogree'). This great triangle of sheer rock and ice slices out of the

Karakoram in awesome isolation – almost 100 miles of frozen desert surrounds it – situated as it is on the border between Pakistan and China. Temperatures here are much colder than Everest, further south. It may not be subjected to the regular monsoons of Nepal but I was only too aware that it suffers wild swings in weather. Even on clear days the wispy streamers of gauzy cloud around the peak are testament to the jet winds that whip round the summit at hundreds of miles an hour. Our journey could involve up to ten days of trekking from Askoli, the last footprint of civilisation on the north-east frontier of Pakistan, to reach a point where we could see K2.

Clearly, altitude is a worry for anyone trekking in this area. The lack of oxygen at these heights can have life-threatening effects if not treated quickly enough – the human body can start to feel altitude at 2000 metres (around 6500 feet). Anyone can be affected by Acute Mountain Sickness – or AMS as it is usually known – but there is no evidence that children are more at risk than adults. The symptoms may at first appear indistinguishable from fatigue, stress and dehydration, but can ultimately prove fatal if left untreated. The key to avoiding problems is to take time to acclimatize, to take plenty of liquids and not to get stressed out and anxious. The problem with children is that the standard drugs used to treat AMS are too powerful, except in the most dire emergency. If AMS was to strike Tom or Kate, my only option would be to lose altitude. I would have to take them much lower, and fast.

I knew what this would involve as we had had one scare like this on our Everest expedition. We had been at Gorak Shep in Nepal, the last tea-house before the Khumbu glacier and base camp, at an altitude of 5160 metres (16 929 feet). Kate had been in a foul mood all day and all she wanted was cuddles from her mum. We sat down to dinner. 'Mummy, I feel sick,' Kate whispered in Alison's ear. Alison bustled her outside just in time as Kate promptly threw up. Andy Pollard, a paediatrician and climber with our partner expedition, the British Mount Everest Medical Expedition, had kindly gone out with them to see if he could be of assistance. 'My head hurts,' Kate complained.

Andy had once gone through the harrowing experience of watching a French trekker die from AMS because his fellow guide thought he knew better than the doctor. He examined Kate closely. 'It may just be something she has eaten – or it could be AMS,' he concluded tentatively.

Alison's maternal instincts switched immediately to overdrive. 'I think we should take her down the mountain,' she said, her mind already made up. The last place where we could be absolutely sure that Kate had been comfortable was Pheriche, 880 metres (2887 feet) below us and at least eight miles away. Andy agreed that prevention was always better than cure. That was enough for Alison; without waiting, she hitched Kate onto her back and was off down the track. She must have been operating on adrenaline for she had not eaten and was still not fully acclimatized. It took the Sherpa, Tenzing, who was supposed to carry Kate down through the night, several miles at a run to catch up with her. By now the pleasant afternoon had turned into steady rain. I packed our basic requirements in a rucksack and set off with our sirdar (leader), Siala, along with Andy and a Sherpa, Zeed, who was carrying Tom. The rain froze into sleet as we crashed down through the scree- and rock-strewn track in darkness, knowing that Alison and Kate were somewhere in front of us. All my thoughts were for the safety of my then three-year-old daughter. Hours later we spotted the flickering lights of the little four-lodge hamlet Lobuche. We had descended 380 metres (1247 feet). Exhausted, we piled through the lodge door to find a smiling Alison and a relaxed and sleepy Kate sitting around the glowing pot-bellied stove. After a few mugs of steaming hot chocolate we decided to play safe and continue our descent to Pheriche, even though Kate looked and felt fully recovered. We arrived tired and exhausted after a journey that had taken most of the night. Whether Kate really had AMS or just a stomach upset we will never know but neither Tom nor Kate suffered any further ill effects as we slowly re-made our ascent. It was an evening I would hate to have to go through again.

I insisted we take doctors to K2. Cath and David Collier were with us on the medical expedition when we journeyed to Everest and had become friends. They knew the children and, more importantly, Tom and Kate liked them. David, 6 feet tall and built like a prop forward – although he destroyed the tough image with his concerned demeanour – was to look after everyone else. He had a great love of mountains and was to be the altitude specialist. His quiet and unassuming wife Cath was to pay particular attention to Tom and Kate. Cath and I had both suffered a bout of giardia, an appalling form of diarrhoea, on our last trip together and if anything brings you close, a shared illness like that does. I remember thinking how dreadful she looked as we struggled along – until, that is, I spotted my reflection in a window and realized I had the same awful grey pallor and sunken cheeks. Cath and David came up from their home in London a few days early to stay at Stone Cottage so that the children would feel comfortable with them by the time we left. It didn't take long before Kate had weaved her usual charm and was sitting on Cath's knee, chatting away as though they had been bosom buddies all their lives.

Roger Courtiour went ahead to Pakistan to smooth the way with the authorities there. Matters were greatly helped by the fact the Pakistani Prime Minister, Benazir Bhutto, took a personal interest in the trip. A statement put out over the international news agency Reuters on the day before we left showed just how much support the Pakistani Government was prepared to give us. It was an unexpected gesture and welcomed by all those closely involved with our journey.

Islamabad, 22 September – The husband and children of British climber Alison Hargreaves are planning to trek to K2, the Himalayan mountain on which she died in Pakistan last month, a Government statement said on Friday. It said Hargreaves' husband James Ballard and their two children, six-year-old Thomas and four-year-old Katherine, were coming at the invitation of Prime Minister Benazir Bhutto.

Bhutto has also ordered a monument to be built in memory of Hargreaves, whose body has not been recovered. The monument will be constructed during Ballard's trip, the statement said. Ballard and his party will fly to Islamabad on Sunday before starting a memorial trek to the base camp on the 8611-metre (28 250-feet) K2, the world's second highest mountain.

Hargreaves, who last May became the first woman to climb Mount Everest alone and without oxygen, perished in snowstorms and icy gales after reaching the summit of K2 on 13 August.

Five other Western climbers went missing and died on K2 the same day, while a sixth succumbed the next day to pulmonary oedema, brought on by the altitude.

Ballard and his children will be accompanied by doctors and a television crew from the British Broadcasting Corporation.

The British High Commission was also eager to help. The main problem was getting everything organized quickly enough. A few weeks delay and the route would be impassable as the bad weather closed in for winter. We were already well beyond the end of the normal commercial trekking season.

Our departure date was established as 23 September. Within days, all the baggage and equipment required for our expedition was delivered to Stone Cottage. Before that I had to make a couple of trips down south, as I had been invited to discuss Alison's and my lifestyle and views on parenthood on a number of television talk shows. I decided I could fit in only two. I did not want to leave Tom and Kate behind, even with a nanny, at a time like this.

On the first occasion, getting off at Euston to do the *The Crystal Rose Show* for Carlton Television, I was touched when a smartly suited young man grabbed my hand. 'I just wanted to say how sorry I was to hear of Alison's death on K2,' he shouted above the railway clatter, before disappearing back into the crowd. Tom and Kate did not even notice him; they were too taken with the rush-hour bustle around them. On our second foray, this time to Norwich to be interviewed by Vanessa Feltz for Anglia, I thought Francesca Shashkova, a free-fall parachutist on the show, summed up admirably the case for professional working mothers with the incisive retort, 'Women are much more than simply grow bags'.

A few days before our departure we met the BBC crew who were to accompany us on the trip in a cosy little Fort William waterfront restaurant. The producer/director, Chris Terrill, looked earnest and dedicated while cameraman Chris Openshaw came across as a bon viveur, disguising a steely strength and determination. Sound man Adrian Bell was quieter than his colleagues but was quickly christened 'Ding Dong' by Kate. They were assisted by Andy Thompson who was universally known as 'Boy'. As the junior, his broad shoulders and big grin had to take the blame for whatever went wrong, whether he was responsible or not.

We were joined by Dave and Cath Collier and Cally Fleming and Ian Sutherland who were also coming to K2 with us. Cally, used to world travel and the outdoor life, was to do any media liaison required. Her fitness for the trip was never in doubt. She was a committed all-round skier and member of the British Telemark Ski Team. Ian 'Suds' Sutherland, one of my oldest friends, was to be our safety officer. It was reassuring to know we had someone with such experience on the team; he had been leader of the local Lochaber mountain rescue team for a over a decade. Tom and Kate began to get tired so I left the gathering to take them home, reflecting as I drove that things boded well for our trip.

Saturday 23 of September arrived quickly and, our big green tote bags finally packed, we sat down to a last evening meal at Stone Cottage. The four-man BBC crew were in attendance as I stirred up the children's favourite pasta dish. Tom and Kate had been photographed and filmed many times in the past with their mother but this was the first time we had invited the cameras into our home. Even so, they took it in their stride, although it was a bit cramped with everybody squeezed into our long thin kitchen. Despite the description 'fly on the wall' we could never forget when the cameras were on us. However, I felt we all got on well and were relaxed in each other's company – indeed, their presence was to become an integral part of the trip.

Climbing on board the sleeper at Fort William station we found the train unusually crowded. 'Can I have something to eat, Dad?' We had just dumped our overnight rucksacks on our berths when Tom made his plaintive cry. The compact cabin offered nothing but complimentary toothpaste and a bottle of water so, as the carriages rattled slowly out of the station and under the evening spread of Ben Nevis's long shadow, we clambered back out into the corridor and fought our way down to the restaurant car.

'Sorry, the restaurant car is not connected, sir,' said the one steward on duty. He informed us he was manning what could only euphemistically be called a 'buffet car'. Food would not be served for another twenty minutes. Fortunately, two charming young women who had taken a break from jobs in London to explore the Hebrides came to our rescue. They offered to swap us some crisps and buttered malt loaf for a couple of gins and tonics. One look at Tom's and Kate's hungry faces and I readily accepted. They wolfed these morsels down quickly as we drew into our local Spean Bridge station, a few miles down the line. Some friends, Nicola and Gavin, who have children at the same nursery as Kate, had been celebrating their wedding anniversary in the converted station restaurant. They rushed out to wave goodbye, poured me a glass of wine which I downed on the platform, presented Tom and Kate with presents for the journey and planted a few 'good luck' kisses. Soon we were off again, rattling slowly towards the bleak but beautiful moonscape of Rannoch Moor for our long haul through the Scottish Highlands to Glasgow and down south.

Tom and Kate then dithered over where they wanted to sleep. Tom played safe and stayed with me, while Kate snatched a much softer option and asked to remain with Cally. Both settled down well and I also found it a comfortable night's sleep. All too quickly we were being awoken by our steward with trays of coffee and biscuits. Outside, the hills and desolate moorland had been replaced by the rolling fields of the home counties. By the time I had Tom and Kate dressed we were pulling into Euston Station in London.

We climbed out stiffly and made our way down to the guard's van to collect our equipment, only to find it locked. An efficient-looking station duty manager approached; unfortunately, she had not come with a key. 'You can't film here,' she pointed out to Chris Terrill. 'No-one told us you were coming. You can't do that here unless you have a permit.' Sudsy, who had wandered off, chose this moment to return dragging a large flat luggage trolley behind him. The duty manager looked at him. 'You can't use that,' she said sternly. 'It's for station personnel only.'

Suddenly we heard a whoop of delight from the main station concourse. It was the London press pack in full cry. They had spotted us and were heading in our direction at a run. The duty manager now had other worries. The BBC crew grabbed the moment to continue filming and managed to find a way to open the guard's van and retrieve the bags and blue plastic barrels containing our equipment. They were hurriedly stacked onto Sudsy's filched trolley as the children and I posed for pictures.

We crossed London to Heathrow. At Terminal Three we were ushered by our hosts, Pakistan International Airlines, into their 'Shalimar' lounge and fed sandwiches and cream cakes. They did not ask for our tickets or passes; clearly we were getting the VIP treatment. PIA's senior management all turned up to see us off. Only their European Manager, who had accidentally been knocked down by Alison as she fled from an over-eager journalist on her last journey home, failed to put in an appearance. Apparently all he had wanted to do was to shake Alison's hand; instead he found himself run over by her size-six boots with her full 9½-stone weight behind them.

Tom and Kate, who were loving the attention being lavished on them by the PIA staff, shivered with anticipation as we boarded the jumbo jet to take us east. Once aboard, they were pampered ridiculously by the stewardesses and before long they had also managed to wangle their way into the cockpit alongside the captain and crew. The jets roared into life at 6.00 p.m. exactly and we took to the air. We had most of business class to ourselves so we settled into luxury for the night. Even Tom and Kate, who were still running on their excitement, wound down enough to go to sleep.

It seemed no time at all before we were tucking into a light breakfast and watching the dawn break on the skyline. A slim horizontal brushstroke of burnt orange was slashed across the dividing line between the black and the blue. The dusty landscape of north-eastern Pakistan rose out of the night-time gloom to meet us.

CHAPTER THREE

A PRIME MINISTER BECKONS

'Come hither! Gentle, fleeting feet,
— Not in response to my prayer
But thro' the promptings of your own dear heart
Riven — with infinite desire.'

MIRZA ASADULA KHAN GHALIB

Economy-class passengers were the first to disembark at Islamabad airport and be hustled into the usual transit buses, after which first class was then emptied into a deluxe model. Only when everyone else had been removed from the aircraft was our party allowed to leave. We stepped out into the sticky morning air, Tom and Kate first with me following, as an air-conditioned coach with tinted windows slipped into place at the bottom of the steps. Clearly our special treatment was to continue. The silent engines purred the few yards to the main terminal building where, instead of joining the usual immigration checks and waiting for baggage reclaim, we were ushered through a small courtyard scattered with potted palms and posted with a couple of armed sentries. Doors opened and we were led into a spacious hall to be served iced drinks, sandwiches and sticky cakes. Tom and Kate took all this for granted and tucked in without hesitation. We hadn't seen our passports since handing them over to Cally in Fort William, days before. Our luggage seemed to have disappeared into the ether.

After these refreshments a second door at the far end of the hall opened and we trooped through to find ourselves in a dusty, exhaust fume-filled car park. Chaos appeared to reign. Hundreds of people were milling about and our totes and barrels were all over the place. Sudsy, concerned but calm, was counting the baggage. The BBC Boy was having a much more frantic time as he tried to keep track of all the bits and pieces of spare film and equipment. The reassuring face of Roger Courtiour, who had been smoothing over details of our trip with the Pakistani authorities for the past week, materialized before me in his familiar cloud of cigarette smoke. 'Welcome to Islamabad,' he shouted above the din, shaking my hand warmly. He was there with a line of guests to whom Tom, Kate and I were to be introduced but, before they could do so, the dignitaries were forced to step aside as yet another swarm of porters descended noisily and planted more totes, bags and plastic drums at our feet. I tried to shake hands with everybody while jumping around to photograph the scene. From there we were led to a minibus which, I was amazed to learn, had been set aside for our private use. We were to find our driver sleeping outside our hotel room whenever he was not behind the wheel.

The BBC crew, Sudsy, Cally, David, Cath, Tom, Kate and I piled on board as the vehicle coughed into life. A short drive took us on to a long straight road and our first real views of northern Pakistan. The lanes were packed with brightly coloured minivans – the type seen most often as delivery vans in Britain – which were used as taxis. They were covered in fairy lights, chrome, mirrors, chocolate-box painted scenes and filled to overflowing, but even when empty the young bloods seemed to prefer to hang like cowboys on the outside. Beside them, horse-drawn carts trotted alongside the latest four-wheel drive vehicles.

It was 7.00 a.m. and the modern grid-plan streets of Islamabad were buzzing. This thirty-year-old city is reminiscent of many modern American cities and, like them, lacks a main centre. We drove through suburb after suburb without a single old building in sight. Everything shouted prosperity. However, the view from our minibus window changed gradually as we moved into Rawalpindi, just over 9 miles away. The once-great colonial city creaked with decaying charm, even though it is today the headquarters of Pakistan's frighteningly efficient army.

All life spilled onto the streets from dark enticing shops, while heavy wooden doors opened invitingly onto twisting alleyways or leafy enclosed courtyards. Makeshift fruit and vegetable markets broke out onto the pavements in a splash of red, yellow and green. It was rush hour as we passed packed buses, workers hailing taxis, smartly dressed schoolchildren marching in rows on their way to class and women wearing bright headscarves bargaining aggressively over early-morning groceries.

As guests of the Pakistani Government we had been lodged in Flashman's Hotel. We drove through a once grand entrance – the gates themselves had long gone – and came to an abrupt halt in front of a long, low, colonial-style building, its whitewashed façade now a peeling yellow. Walking through the portals of this venerable institution was like taking a step back seventy years. At one time the hotel, situated amid a startling green expanse of gardens and bubbling streams, was an oasis of luxury for the pampered rich. Since then, the years have taken their toll: the columned front entrance has been denuded of rich ornaments and the electricity and plumbing remain basic at best. However in Asia the Flashman still retains an enormous reputation and undoubted charm. The deep club armchairs, heavy mahogany furniture and elaborate wall coverings have barely been touched since the 1920s, while the attentiveness of the starch-suited staff, who waited on us hand and foot, is also an indulgent throwback to a more romantic era. We could not have been better looked after; everyone down to the dobhi-wallah (laundryman) belonged to yesteryear. For less than the price of a packet of cigarettes he laundered clothing for four adults and two children and returned it so well-ironed that even the socks were smartly creased and Kate's kilt had been completely re-pleated.

As we tumbled into the lobby we were relieved to see a smartly dressed waiter approaching with a tray heaving under the weight of mugs and sweet buns. It was an incredibly hot and sticky day and we all made a grab for the drinks until Cath, our strict health advisor, took one look at the thick milky concoction and gave us a stern rebuke. The tray was whisked away and some safer bottled soft drinks were ordered.

I was slightly baffled when Tom, Kate and I were shown along the passage and into a vast room filled with sofas, elegant desks, tables and chairs – but no beds. I wandered down to the other end and opened a great set of double doors. Before me was a cool, dark, tree-lined courtyard. Tom and Kate clattered through this private garden and only when we had worked our way to the far end did I find another set of apartments with an enormous bed for me and smaller ones for the children. We had been allocated the original presidential suite!

Alison, I learned later from her diaries (recovered from base camp), had stayed at the Hotel Shalimar. Her time in Rawalpindi three months earlier had obviously been hectic.

Tuesday 13 June. Given rooms, baggage taken upstairs, crashed out. Had been asleep half an hour when the phone rang. It was a reporter, desperate to be the first for an interview. Agreed to give him one…to the deputy British high commissioner's house for tea. It was primarily a reception for people to meet me. Consequently I had to welcome guests on arrival…Drinks, chat, tea and speeches. Invited to a party that evening and I quickly asked around about dress. I was told it was uniforms! Joan, the delightful Lancastrian wife of the senior vice-president of the Pakistani Alpine Club, Daud Beg, took me under her wing and drove me first to a dress shop and then to a shoe shop. Bought both within five minutes and spent one thousand rupees (about twenty pounds). Felt smarter and much happier. To their house for a shower and chat and then to the party for 8.00 p.m. Very social. Back to the hotel for 11.00 p.m.

No-one had slept well on the night flight over, mainly through excitement and anticipation, so we all opted for an easy morning until we joined the BBC crew for lunch at the nearby Pearl Continental Hotel. Later, with the crew in tow, we set out to explore the city around us, heading first for the marketplace, or Naya Bazaar as it is called. Modern Pakistan dropped away as we snatched our first glimpses of the pounding heart of old Rawalpindi. The twisting alleys had hardly altered in several hundred years and the disintegrating stone buildings on either side hung over them so precariously that they seemed to touch above our heads as we weaved through the motley display of goods that spilled out under our feet. Young boys, many no older than Tom, were sitting cross-legged and hammering away at their work but my six-year-old son could no more draw a comparison between his life and theirs than he could with little green men on Mars.

A delicious aroma lured us into the tea section of the bazaar, where wrinkled and grinning tradesmen pushed polished but worn brass scoops containing samples of their favoured blends up to our noses. Suddenly our senses would be transported to Bangladesh, Ceylon or China. I noticed the absence of one of the great tea-growing nations and committed my first major faux pas by enquiring, 'Do you have any India tea?' The reply was a curt, 'Sir, we do not like to have anything to do with that place.' It was definitely time to move on. The gentle fragrances stayed with us until we reached the next crossroads, where we were hit by the pungent aroma of cumin, chilli and coriander. We had reached the haunt of the spice merchants and the smell was overpowering. Sacks of exotic spices gradually changed to dried peas, beans and lentils, each one stacked in rolled-down jute sacks. Much to Tom's and Kate's delight the shopkeepers invited them to run their fingers through these exciting textures. The normally hard-nosed tradesmen were clearly mesmerized by Kate's charm and deep green eyes. She chatted away to them, not caring whether they understood her or not but recognizing she was the centre of attention. Tom, always more reserved, allowed her to take the limelight on that occasion.

In the heart of this bustle was the most affluent section of the great market: the rice stalls. This was fat-cat city, bazaar-style. An almost cathedral-like hush descended as we stepped into the massive wooden warehouses with their stockpiles of this Eastern staple. Normal market chatter was blocked out as the wealthy tradesmen bartered for the best deals across glasses of warm tea and strong cigarettes. Just across the street were a stunning row of ancient Tibetan-style stone houses, their wooden balconies sagging with age but their ornate carvings still evident. They were among the oldest buildings left in the city.

'Dad, Dad,' came a familiar voice. I had been shooting away with my camera when I felt a small hand tugging at my T-shirt. 'Can I have a drink, Dad?' Kate looked worryingly flushed. I took off my rucksack and rummaged inside; no drinks bottle. I appealed to David, Cath, Cally and Sudsy, none of whom had thought to bring any refreshment. In desperation, I even turned to Roger and the film crew but I was met with blank faces. Here we were, only a half day into our trip, and we had already made a fundamental error – we were not carrying drinking water and had a sponge-dry child on our hands. Although there was plenty of refreshment on sale we could not be sure any of these local brews were safe for the children to drink. I spotted a stall selling cans of Pepsi so Roger plunged into his pocket, produced handful of rupees and off we headed in that direction.

We were to be disappointed. The fat stallholder squatting on a low stool would not even sell us a can of drink or two as the boy beside him sneeringly informed us they were wholesalers. We would have to pay for a whole crate or nothing. They were the only two unpleasant Pakistanis we met. Roger and I walked away in frustration but we were growing more concerned about Kate's need for hydration. My young daughter continued to whine in my ear and we decided the best option would be to cut back to the main thoroughfare. The temperature was in the high 80s (31 °C) but in the narrow streets it felt more like 100 °F (37 °C). Luckily there were drink vendors by the score on this stretch and within seconds Kate, Tom and everyone else were guzzling ice-cold bottles of fizz.

Once they had some liquid poured into them, Tom and Kate were content to wander further. Gradually the traders and street hawkers congesting the alleys of the bazaar became fewer and fewer in number and we had a bit of space to stretch our legs and tramp the dusty streets. The road opened out into a large oblong where hundreds of horses harnessed to wooden two-wheel gharries waited patiently in lines, lazily swishing away flies. Their owners took turns to tout for taxi trade. Although thin, the beasts looked well cared for and each had his own nosebag resting on the tailgate of the trap in front. Tucked away in a corner was a blacksmith hammering at a shoe on his anvil. It sent brilliant white shards of metal flying through his workshop gloom. I felt a nostalgic twinge watching this little artisan practise his ancient art while polluting Japanese vans flew along the road behind me.

'Can I be carried, Dad?' A plaintive voice interrupted my thoughts. It was Kate again, her attention span finally beginning to wane. We decided it was time to head back to the hotel. Cally took the children for an evening swim at the Pearl, but by the time I caught up with them it was dusk and the mosquitoes had descended. I took one look at the cloud of buzzing black insects and decided not to run even the outside risk of catching malaria. Instead, we had a quick dinner and then it was off to bed. Kate decided to spend the night in Cally's room again so Tom and I settled down to the luxury of our enormous spread in the presidential suite. Hot and sweaty, I grappled in the flickering electric light with an ornate but temperamental shower, only grasping how it worked as my patience reached breaking point. I had to turn it on, leave it for just over half an hour – by which time it had finally warmed up – before jumping in, washing as quickly as possible and darting out again before it started to go cold.

The following morning our faithful driver was ready and waiting to take us to the Pearl Continental Hotel. There everybody got out except David and me. The children went off with Cath and Cally for a European-style breakfast and morning swim. David and I were joined by Chris Terrill and we drove to the Holiday Inn to meet Roger Courtiour. Over rolls and coffee we were introduced to the man who was to be our trek guide, Ashraf Aman. Thanks to the good offices of the Pakistani Government we had managed to secure the services of the first Pakistani climber to summit K2.

Ashraf was born and brought up in Hunza, a tiny, land-locked, once-independent kingdom sandwiched between the top of Pakistan and China. It sits right at the end of a section of the ancient trading route, the Silk Road, which runs through the Karakoram to China.

Small and squarely built with crewcut hair and a clipped military moustache, he had the look of a pirate but was the salt of the earth. His broad, spatula-like hands were those of someone who has had to work brutally hard all his life. The tough exterior lived up to the reputation I already knew of the Hunza as a strong, ferocious, but loyal people. Ashraf had put his success on K2 in 1977 to good use by setting up his own trekking company, Adventure Tours Pakistan. He was to provide our porters, cooks, kitchen staff and local food but, from our point of view, most valuable of all was his own local knowledge of the Baltoro area, where we were heading. Extremely polite, courteous and correct, Ashraf would always address me as either 'Mr Jim' or 'Mr James', despite my entreaties to be less formal.

Back out in the bright sunlight our minibus whizzed up and came to a halt before us. We were whisked to the Pakistan Tourism Development Corporation offices where the director, Raja Changez Sultan, a large avuncular man, welcomed us. Educated at Shrewbury, one of England's leading public schools, Changez was urbane and smooth. He was to accompany us to Skardu and quizzed me for hours on the merits of trout fishing in Scotland and the state of the salmon reaches that season. Angling, he informed me, was one of his passions, along with painting, poetry and, of course, cricket. This was protocol day for me. We had to finalize details of the trek and set up permits for the military areas we intended to travel through. Finally, a luncheon was to be held in our honour hosted by the chairman of PTDC, Riaz Hussain Qureshi, and attended by the British high commissioner and his wife.

We went back and picked up the children, who had burned off most of their excess energy in the pool. Together we were driven to the hilltop restaurant overlooking the futuristic expanse of Islamabad and the opulent white marble of the Shah Faisal Mosque. Situated on the side of the Margalla hills, this is purported to be the biggest mosque in Asia and can hold up to 100 000 worshippers. The heat on the hillside was almost unbearable in the midday sun. Tom and Kate, who had been spoiled with enough cola and titbits to sink a battleship during their morning by the pool, were not hungry but were having a great time. Everywhere we went I was to find Pakistan very child-orientated; as soon as both men and women spotted Tom and Kate they could not resist approaching and making friends, reaching out to touch the children's faces in a way they found initially rather startling.

Over lunch Mr Qureshi paid a moving tribute to Alison: 'I would just like to express my feeling at this sad occasion...of course, Mr James, it is not a good time for you because of this incident but I'm very much thankful you spared time and shared your views with us. We, the Pakistanis, also share your concern and feelings about his lady, a very famous mountaineer. And, it can be evident from the gesture of our Prime Minister, Benazir Bhutto, that she has shown her concern and directed all the Government institutions to do all we can for your visit here.'

I felt my thanks were inadequate for the generosity they had shown me, my family and friends and ended my speech by reiterating, 'Alison and I have always lived our life in one way and that is in the light of the old Tibetan saying, "Better to have lived one day as a tiger than a thousand years as a sheep".'

After all the formalities, I was glad to escape for a leisurely swim with Tom and Kate. The pair of them seemed completely unfazed by the heat and new time zone, even though we were four hours ahead of Britain. Our two days in Rawalpindi were nearly over. Roger and I had only to collect the permits and we were ready to go; he back to Britain, the rest of us to Baltistan. Departure for Skardu was set for early next morning.

The two of us had arranged to rejoin the party for an early evening meal at the Pearl. We wandered across the cool marble lobby thinking about downing several chilled cans of non-alcoholic beer when I was approached by a short, olive-skinned man with narrow eyes and a soapy handshake. He introduced himself as Abdul Quddus of Nazir Sabir Expeditions and said he had looked after the American expedition to K2, of which Alison had been a member. 'I was so sorry to hear about Alison. You have my most sincere condolences, most sincere,' he lisped. He moved on rapidly to quiz me about my own party's movements. Clearly, what he wanted to know was whether we would hire him to look after us on our trek and he could not hide his disappointment when I said this had already been arranged. He seemed nervous and ill-at-ease, hopping from one foot to the other as he spoke. 'We have all Alison's equipment recovered from base camp at our stores,' he then announced abruptly. I was surprised. I thought it had been handed over to the British High Commission weeks before. I wanted to find out how we could get hold of it and put it into safekeeping until our return. He explained we could have it at any time. Our brief discussion with Mr Quddus was over and he slipped away as anonymously as he had come. It had been a long day and, as we sank into our seats and ordered drinks, I felt a sense of unease that I had still not seen Alison's belongings.

After dinner we sent our driver home for an early night as he had to drive us to the airport at 4.00 o'clock the next morning. Instead, we all wandered back to Flashman's, where we arrived in the warm evening darkness. Pinned to my hotel door was a message asking me to ring the American Embassy. I dialled on my bedside phone and asked for the attaché named. She was pulled out of a reception to take my call. 'Mr Ballard, how nice to hear you are in Rawalpindi,' she said with a gushing American twang. 'I was trying to contact you to say that we have just had the personal effects of Rob Slater and the other remaining equipment from the American expedition returned. I thought you should know.' I told her what had happened to me that evening. She seemed pleased all the equipment had at last materialized and I felt a bit better about that situation. Before ringing off she added, 'I must say I very much enjoyed meeting Alison when I attended one of her functions on the way to K2. I think it is a fine thing taking the children to the mountain.'

CHAPTER FOUR

A TIME TO JOURNEY

'It is better to travel than arrive.'

ARABIC SAYING

'Are we going in another aeroplane, Dad? Can I sit next to Cath on the plane? Can I, Dad, can I?' The questions came thick and fast as I tried to put my mind in gear. Kate had woken as I took the luggage for our flight to Skardu out into the relative cool of the morning and she was immediately a bundle of energy. It was 4.00 a.m. and the air was alive with the sound of the dawn chorus and the haunting echoes of the muezzins calling the Muslim faithful to prayer. Tom, always more reluctant to be pulled from his slumbers, was grumpy. 'I don't want to have a shower,' he mumbled as I tried to coax him out of bed.

There was a new sense of excitement among the party as we were bused to the airport. Even I, a hardened traveller, felt the childlike sense of anticipation that comes before a step into the unknown. Here we were met by our cheerful PTDC friend Changez, who was accompanying us to Skardu to make sure our trip to K2 and back went as smoothly as possible – a fine gesture by his department.

We arrived at the airport to find delays. The day before there had been an attempt to smuggle a gun through the internal flight section and in the ensuing debacle a passenger was stabbed to death. Armed airport officers known as 'sky marshals' promptly shot and killed the assailant, but it had resulted in a rigorous security clampdown. With our mountain of luggage there was no way we were going to get through the checks without some kind of search. Cath and I were the unfortunate two pulled over. A small security guard glared at us with unveiled suspicion from tiny terrier-like eyes and demanded a female officer be summoned to go through Cath's bag. 'Open this one,' he barked at me. It was the main medical barrel stuffed with the best in modern drugs and equipment. 'I can only do that when the tourism officer is present,' I replied, looking around for Changez. Cath got the same treatment but we stood our ground, resolving not to be bullied by his attitude. There was no need for rudeness and I knew in his mood he would be careless and might damage some of our vital equipment. If looks could kill we would both have been 6 feet under, but there was nothing he could do but wait until Changez turned up. Eventually the barrel was opened and our security guard had a cursory feel before slamming it closed, disappointed. The team's penknives, batteries and clocks had to be handed over as these were considered high-risk articles and were to be put in the safekeeping of the flight crew until we landed in Skardu. The BBC Boy, who had been marching around during all this with a Leatherman – a kit comprising foldable pliers, knife and screwdrivers – hitched to his belt, sparked another bout of paranoia. It was left to Changez to calm them down but, even with his soothing tones, the Leatherman was added to the pile of 'contraband' before we were allowed to board.

The 737 was packed. It was the first flight out of Islamabad to Skardu for a few days because the weather had been too bad to make the hour-long journey without radar – visibility has to be perfect for the flights to be allowed on the route. Electronic guidance equipment is not permitted because airspace over this part of Baltistan has been closely controlled by the Pakistani military since disputes with India broke out over the border areas in 1977. Until then, small aircraft had ploughed back and forth. Now, planes have to be large enough to cope with the unsettled weather conditions. No flight can set off until the crew have been informed landing is possible at Skardu.

The plane climbed slowly above the city haze to reveal gradually unfolding views. At first, all we could see were a series of serrated silhouettes emerging from the early morning mist and cloud. Suddenly, the mountains jumped out at us, looking as if they had been

cut out of a sheet of steel and simply tacked in a row one behind the
other ad infinitum. Nanga Parbat, a 8125-metre (26 660-feet) peak
out on its own, sat like a massive vanilla scoop on an ice-cream cornet.
Chris Terrill tapped on my shoulder. 'The flight crew suggest you
might like to look in the cockpit,' he said.

'Would you like that kids?' I asked Tom and Kate.

'Yeah!' they shouted in unison.

The pilot and co-pilot smiled over their shoulders as the children
and I slipped in behind them. I crouched on the navigator's seat, my
head bent to avoid the low ceiling and to allow Tom, who was behind
me, to see over. Kate was in front, standing between my doubled-up
knees. The two rectangular windows were filled from side to side with
a sea of snowy peaks. Haramosh and its satellites were in the centre
and there, above a field of minnows and to the right, was the perfect
mighty grey-and-white pyramid of K2. Slicing into the blue skies, it
was unmistakable. Even at that distance it simply dominated all other
mountains on the horizon.

'Kate, look out of this window. See that white triangle? That's
K2,' I whispered. Kate's little face stared hard at the icy monolith
before her but she said nothing. Tom, startled, pressed close against
me as he peered outside. He had the film crew behind him, who were
all anxiously trying to look out of the cockpit window. I felt his breath
against my beard. 'Yes, Tom, that is K2, your mum's last mountain.'
He looked but, like his sister, said nothing. There was nothing to say.
For all of us it was a moment to drink in nature's power. All you could
hear was the clicking of the flight-control panel and the faint whir of
the cameras.

Alison's diaries were to reveal that, three months earlier, she had
sat in the same cockpit looking out over the same views:

*Wednesday 14 June. Recognized by a PIA pilot who had seen me on the
BBC and he offered me a flight in the cockpit. So after a light meal I
went up front and sat and chatted and took photographs. Brilliant! I was
even made to stay up front for the landing. Grand!*

I led a thoughtful Tom and Kate back to their seats as the others made their way forward to look at the mountain we had all come to see. I clipped them back into their seatbelts and sunk back into my own seat beside them. I could not get our first view of mighty K2 out of my mind. It was an overpowering image; much more impressive in its own way than the huge bulk of Everest, which sits in a range of mountains of similar height while K2 stands alone. In just over five weeks since their mother's death I had been able to fulfil my promise to my children. I had shown them where their mother had triumphed and been killed. It may only have been out of an aeroplane window but, if all else failed, at least they had seen it. Nature had been on our side. I had known we would pass close enough to the Karakoram to see K2 during the flight but nine times out of ten the weather closes in and the range is obscured by a wet wall of grey cloud.

The rest of the flight passed quickly and the plane was soon descending to Skardu. As it banked our view changed and we curved down over the browns and ochres of the desert, watching the rolling smaller peaks on the right swing into the Haramosh range and then round again so that we were looking over the Karakoram. Underneath us was the Indus, bending serpentine-like along its wide beige riverbed. The frontier town of Skardu was hidden by a massive volcanic plug of rock that forces the rising Indus into yet another huge twist, just at the point where it is joined by the Shigar river carrying water from the melting snow of K2. The military-built runway sits amid this high sand- and rock-strewn landscape at 2350 metres (7600 feet). This has to be, without doubt, the most beautiful and moving commercial airline flight in the world.

The film crew jumped out in front of us as soon as we landed to catch us as we came out of the plane but they were intercepted by a handful of stern-looking security men who told them in no uncertain terms that filming was not allowed. Inside the terminal we were packed into a tiny room for a tea ceremony, which, I began to realise, was a ritual to expect before or after every journey. So many civic dignitaries had been ordered out to meet us that they had to wait outside and take turns. Tom and Kate became the centre of attention as usual so I was able to gulp down some refreshing jasmine tea and nibble on the bite-size sweetmeats. Outside we were led to a line of waiting Japanese-manufactured four-wheel drive vehicles. I had been presented with a soft-iced cake by the PIA managing director as we left the aircraft, which was balanced precariously on my knee, but my attempts to keep the cake in one piece became difficult as we hiccuped over pothole after pothole on the bumpy tarmac.

Bubbling water churned inside a carefully built channel, which ran along both sides of the road on its way to irrigation ditches in nearby fields, private plots and even to individual trees. I was amazed at how the water from the Indus was used with such care to turn this desert land into one that can produce apricots, apples, tomatoes and even melons. Small goats picked away at tufts of greenery in between broken walls, pulling the last leaves from ragged bushes, while their tiny minders waved big sticks and threw stones to keep them on the move. Houses were nothing more than a flat roof covering a small square patch of ground with only the more affluent ones having a mud-brick wall of sorts.

Our vehicles squeezed past the others on the road except for the army jeeps, whose drivers insisted on their right of way as we approached Skardu proper. In recent years the area has been dominated by Pakistan's armed forces and this was evident everywhere we went. Skardu, the ancient capital of the Baltistan region (where the now trendy Balti curry originated from) was once the centre of a powerful kingdom in its own right and the castle still remains on the volcanic hillside overlooking the river and valley. It is a hardy and peculiarly individual breed of hill people who have survived the centuries up there. The high summer temperatures are enough to fry your brains, while in winter the surface of the Indus can freeze completely and the locals use it to walk from one bank to the other. Luckily, we were travelling in neither extreme.

Our vehicles ground into low gear as the road climbed steeply and Skardu began. The simple huts turned to single-storey terraced shop fronts. Everything from plumbing equipment to dresses was on haphazard display, with much of the stock piled on the roofs in large wheelbarrows. The mountains, all greys and browns, loomed nearer than ever behind them; their sides eroded and twisted by the arteries of dry stream beds that turn to raging torrents when the snows melt. Closer in, alleyways leading off from the main roads showed glimpses of the real town and its centuries-old way of life.

We pulled up at the K2 Motel, where virtually every trekker or climber wants to stay before moving into the mountains. Consequently a few tourist shops have sprung up on its doorstep. We ate my slightly knocked-about cake on the lawn and washed it down with more tea as we lapped up the views – we were on a terrace high above the Indus flood plain – before checking in. Sher Ali, the motel's manager, clad in the traditional shalwar qamiz – two-piece cotton trousers and long shirt top – approached and shook my hand. 'Mr Ballard, it is so very nice to meet you,' he said. 'We have kept room twelve for you and your family as it was the one Alison stayed in on her way into K2.' The staff obviously derived pleasure from giving us Alison's room but it had been so long since she had used it, so many people had been there in between and hotel rooms are designed to be impersonal anyway, that there was nothing of her presence when we moved in. Even so, as they walked through the door Tom remarked unusually, 'This is nice'. Both he and Kate then sat quietly as I unpacked. The room had big high ceilings, with a large wooden bed and walk-in wardrobes. Alison had noted in her diary:

Thursday 15 June. The K2 Motel – a lovely place; quiet, peaceful, relaxing, clean and wholesome. Beautiful gardens and view over the Indus river. It is great to be here. Pakistan is a far nicer place than I expected. The people are kind and helpful and Skardu, particularly this place, is a delight.

We were to spend three days here acclimatizing, so after lunch we decided to go exploring and get some exercise after our flight. We chose to visit Satpara lake, reached by a hair-raising jeep ride along a steep rutted dirt track. This levelled out as we ran alongside a clear rushing river shadowed by fine old trees. It was a beautiful spot, strangely European in look, and I made the jeeps stop so I could take some pictures. Much to our chagrin we could barely find a space in the car park a few miles further on as it was packed with chauffeur-attended military jeeps. After squeezing our convoy in, we crossed the road and scrambled down to the lake shore. Here we found the whole area stuffed with more gold braid and stars than on a wedding cake. Clearly this was a popular place for army chiefs to come and unwind. They did not look at all pleased to see our merry band, particularly Tom and Kate. Obviously they thought they had the place to themselves for the afternoon. Just in sight, but out of hearing, were their wives and daughters who came across eager to speak and were happy to chat away about our visit. In their clipped English they told me how they had all followed Alison's story on television and in the newspapers and wished us well with our adventure. I was conscious that I was the only one, as a Yorkshireman, to drop my aitches.

Before we left they kindly offered to take us on a boat ride around the lake but we had to pass on that because they could not find any life jackets that fitted the children. Instead we continued down the hillside to the small hamlet of Satpara, where there were reported to be fine rock carvings. A rickety old bridge made from wooden poles lashed together with rusty cable led across a swirling stream and allowed us to scramble up the loose rocks to see these images of the meditating Buddha, the intricacies of which had sadly been eroded on most of them by the harsh climate. We returned to our vehicles and back to Skardu for an early night. Tom and Kate went to bed without another mention of their first view of Mum's last mountain...

CHAPTER FIVE

INSHALLAH

Pilgrim remember
For all your pain
The Master you seek abroad
You will find at home —
Or walk in vain.

ANON

Tom and Kate were curled up and still snuffling into their duvets as I slipped out of the large double bed. A faint golden glow was just beginning to seep through the shuttered windows. I dressed and made my way along the corridor to the terrace, camera in hand. Sudsy was already sitting there, hands behind the back of his head, drinking in the early morning light. 'Look at this — a mountain range that climbers' dreams are made of,' he declared as I took it all in, amazed at another day of clear blue skies. In front of us the terrace dropped steeply away to the flood plain below, which stretched for several miles on either side of the milky-green Indus, the great river known as the 'cradle of civilization' that rises in Tibet, flows around the Himalayas and through Pakistan. As we watched, the sun crept across it, changing the colour from dark khaki to chalk white. It would be months before the snows melted and swelled the river to a raging torrent covering the flat sands once more. Beyond the valley was the Haramosh range, every crease and gully etched boldly in the light.

It was great to see one of my oldest friends cast aside his usual Highland reserve and relax in the beauty around us. Suds and I had met climbing in the Italian Dolomites in 1966 and spent a weekend of rest and relaxation in Venice when the weather closed in. Since then we had climbed with each other irregularly and now – lured by the Scottish mountains – I lived just a few miles from him and his wife, another Catherine. He was someone to be relied upon, even in the most arduous circumstances.

The only sound that morning was a muffled chipping as the workmen below us dug new terraces into the steep hillside. They were hacking their way through a pile of rocks, chiselling them into shape and fitting them neatly into the dry-stone walls supporting the flattened earth. Their concentration and expertise reminded me of similar work I had seen in the Peak District over 7000 miles away in England. As in previous centuries, all they had to help them were simple hand tools such as shovels, picks, crowbars, hammers and cold chisels. However, times are changing. The terraces were being created to make an overflow camp site for the motel as more and more trekking expeditions head along this, until recently little-used, route. With wise forward planning the Pakistan Tourism Development Corporation are trying to prevent the pollution caused to the environment by unregulated camping.

Changez explained their concern about this new growth in visitors over dinner one night. 'There are two great secrets in Pakistan: one is our nuclear programme, the other is our tourist potential. Everyone knows about our nuclear programme but no-one knows about our beautiful country. The struggle for countries like ours is that there is always a conflict between the amount of development wanted by the people and needed by society and the amount of land that should be put aside for "green" areas. There is a sense that it is important to leave things in their natural state. Our main concern is mass tourism and the damage it can bring.'

Leaving Sudsy on the terrace, I went to round up the others for breakfast. David, an early riser, was already off with his cameras. I knocked on Cally's door, aware she was always reluctant to get out of bed in the morning. 'I was just coming to meet you,' she said when she finally answered, still in her nightshirt and with dishevelled hair. I was unconvinced. Tom and Kate dressed and went to wake Cath and we all breakfasted on chapattis, jam and fried eggs.

A short jeep ride took us to the bazaar. The BBC crew wanted to film the children and me pottering about. This is something Alison would not have enjoyed. On the whole she disliked travel and would much rather have been dropped at the base of her chosen mountain, if that had been possible, instead of making the long journey each overseas climb invariably involved. Only Tibet and the Tibetans had interested her, although her journey through Baltistan, I discovered later from her diaries, also left a favourable impression:

Friday June 16. I enjoyed the flowers, the views, the rivers and their old rickety suspension bridges made from wood, with their impressive gorges and undercut roads.

The bazaar was no tourist haunt but the everyday shopping centre for the whole of Baltistan. No matter what you wanted, you could buy it here, from the traditional flat-topped felted wool Baltistan cap – the nating – with its distinctive rolled rim, to the latest plumbing accessory, the ballcock. At last we heard the words, 'It's a wrap' and Tom, Kate and I were able to squeeze our way through the curious onlookers and find some relative anonymity. With the film crew in tow it had been impossible not to attract attention but now we were able to slip quietly through the streets with only the odd pair of inquisitive eyes following us. I enjoyed the mundane nature of these everyday scenes. One long dog-legged alley was full of iron-workers and tailors. Here the blacksmiths worked the red-hot iron between primitive anvil and hammer. Without benches, all their work had to be carried out on the hard earth floor while the power for the bellows was provided by a hand-turned Heath Robinson-type contraption that masqueraded as an air pump. It worked extremely well and the charcoal glowed white-hot. Eager young boys working in the shadows even moved their old Singer sewing machines around so that I could photograph them stitching away in the best natural light.

As arranged we rejoined the rest of the team a couple of hours later, only to find that Cath had not turned up and David had organized a sweep of the rambling bazaar. We trooped back down the street of tailors and heard a European voice saying, 'Take fifty rupees off that and I'll buy it'. Cath was bargaining for all she was worth over a particularly stylish nating. Time had been forgotten as she purchased with the same vengeance as the locals, much to the amusement of the shopkeepers, who were not prepared to give her an extra inch. Few Balti women are seen shopping in this Islamic society but both Cath and Cally were quite happy to wander alone for hours without any hassle from anyone.

Shangri-la — that fabled heavenly paradise on earth — was supposed to exist in deepest darkest Tibet but, according to a signpost on the road from the airport to Skardu, it was just 18 kilometres (11 miles) away. I decided this was worth investigating during our three-day stay in this frontier town, especially as our party had been provided with government jeeps. We left the bazaar behind and our small convoy rattled off up the steep route. Tom and Kate were happy to travel in the basic four-wheel drives. They loved the painful groans coming from the rest of the assembled team as we jolted along the treacherous but breathtaking routes. They themselves had the soft cradle of either my, Cath's or Cally's lap to cushion their bouncing bodies. Locals have a saying here that jeep drivers can make one mistake in their career — they never get the chance to make two. On roads like this, I could see why.

Sure enough there it was, 'Shangri-la', painted clearly on the roadside sign. We rolled through holiday camp-style high walls into a Japanese scene that would not have looked out of place in Kyoto. Little red-roofed pagodas dotted an immaculately tended Japanese water garden, complete with wooden arch bridges and weeping willows. This Shangri-la was specifically designed to be a playground for the rich. Personally, I found this artifice and manipulation of nature an inappropriate contrast in an environment where the beauty lay in its untamed wilderness. We stayed for a coffee on the veranda overlooking a perfectly manicured lawn and lake. In front of us was a fuselage from an American DC3 warplane, now converted into the resort's 'honeymoon suite'. Kate and Tom were warm and dusty from the drive and the placid lake in front of them proved an irresistible attraction. As I tried to sip my freshly ground coffee they gave me no peace. 'Dad, Dad, can I have a swim?' Their questioning voices rose higher until I gave in and we all wandered down to the water's edge so that the pair could splash about to their heart's content before we left.

As we spiralled upwards our route passed tiny villages hanging with difficulty on their own little plateaus covered in the local speciality, apricots. These fruits – sold overseas as Hunza apricots – are part of the Balti staple diet and are used to make curries, oils and sweets. Locals believe the fruit can enhance a long life and help acclimatization. The road began to disintegrate and at one point we had to stop, climb out and clear some boulders to prevent us slipping into an irrigation channel.

Driving through one high mountain hamlet we came across a class of children, no older than Tom, packing the road in front of us. They giggled and danced down the street in their traditional shalwar qamis. We climbed out to see what was going on. I looked the real tourist in T-shirt and slacks with cameras around my neck and Tom in one hand and Kate in the other. Carefully circumventing the gathering, we found a space between their bobbing heads and saw they had congregated around a bullock. It was lying on its side, bound above the hooves with crude sisal rope. Quickly I realized what was going on; these youngsters had been brought out of school to witness the rare slaughter of one of the village's beasts. Islamic culture demands the ritual bleeding to death of any animal for consumption. I turned to Cally. 'Take the children back to the jeep,' I ordered urgently.

'What?...Why?' She had not yet realized what was happening.

'Just do it, please.'

Cally urged them away. 'I want to stay. Dad, why can't I stay?' pleaded Tom. Kate was happy to go with her friend Cally. 'Go on Tom, I'll tell you later,' I pressed. Reluctantly, he turned and followed the girls up the hill.

The schoolchildren watched the slaughter with as much interest as people in Britain might watch a soap opera on television, but I thought such scenes were definitely not for my vegetarian six- and four-year-olds. A sinewy slaughterman and his lean assistant crouched over the doomed beast. The animal's head was laid across a scooped-out pit in the ground, an enormous silver dagger was produced and in a single, practised movement the slaughterman slit its throat from ear to ear. Blood started pumping in thick gurgling spurts into the earthy bowl and the bullock's life quietly began to ebb away. Within minutes its body became limp and the ceremony was over. The children went back to school and we climbed into the jeeps once more. 'What was it, Dad?' Tom pounced on me eagerly. 'It was a ceremony, Tom, to do with this people's religion.' I grappled for an explanation a six-year-old would understand. 'It involved killing a bullock. They believe that, unless the animal is killed correctly, its meat cannot be fit to eat.' Tom looked at me blankly. It was a far cry from the soya sausages and veggie burgers he was used to seeing on his dinner plate.

In these mountain haunts I was stuck by the isolation of each village. The local people seemed to live within the confines of their few houses and fields. The men had a wild untamed look that suggested a tough outdoor life, while the women were barely seen. Changez, always a fount of information, explained that society in Baltistan, which came under the suzerainty of the modern state of Pakistan with Partition of British India in 1947, was still struggling to come to terms with the modern world. At the tribal or family level it was still very homogeneous, he said, but on the larger scale of government and state it barely clung together. 'So far, the country has not existed long enough and our institutions are not that highly developed to be a cohesive whole. The people here don't know how to "play the game" by these rules. You will see this dichotomy everywhere you go.'

Our ride switched to an upland plain but the vehicles had gone as far as they could. The rutted slots masquerading as a road had finally merged to become nothing more than a narrow, well-worn footpath.

Our drivers pulled over for a much-needed round of cigarettes while the rest of us gathered up our rucksacks and photographic gear and set off on foot along the grassy edges of a former glacial valley. The whole area was reminiscent of the Bregaglia region on the Swiss–Italian border. To one side of us were a couple of wooden farmsteads with fine carved entrance porches and a smattering of goats and sheep but no sign of human life. We rounded some rocky debris and started a zigzag descent to a mountain lake. The first splashes of startling turquoise could be glimpsed through birch trees. An old handmade wooden rowing boat was chained beneath a copse of weeping willows trailing endlessly into an almost perfect oval of water. We dropped our rucksacks on the shingle beach and were pondering whether it was safe to swim when a boy of nine or ten suddenly materialized, shook off his plastic sandals and once-white shalwar qamis and slipped into the clean water for a swim. It was so clear you could see his arms and legs circling frantically beneath the surface as he affected a crude swimming movement somewhere between the crawl and breast stroke. Tom and Kate where stunned someone else had beaten them to it. They looked at me as if to say, 'Why aren't we swimming?' The entire film crew along with Cally immediately volunteered to accompany them into the water – just for safety's sake, of course. It had nothing to do with the fact this refreshing oasis had appeared after several hot sticky hours in our jeeps. I asked one of the tourist officers with us whether swimming would cause any offence. 'Sir, if they are willing to risk being eaten by the lake's monster then we do not mind,' he said with a mischievous smile. Apparently, legend has it that the lake is occupied by something akin to Nessie. I felt that, living as we did not a stone's throw from Loch Ness without ever having had a single sighting of the Scottish beast, it was a risk worth taking. Anyway, I could always send the BBC Boy in first to test the waters and if that did not tempt the monster I was pretty sure that Kate could frighten anything. After a brief swim, lunch called. It was time to dry ourselves and return to Skardu. We had a date with a polo match for the afternoon.

When we reached our jeep, our driver, Jarputra, asked keenly,

'Sir, Mr Jim, are you ready to leave?' and with barely a chance to close the doors his foot was on the accelerator and we shot off along the precarious track. We were bounced and bruised all the way down the mountainside until we reached the last hamlet on the track. Blocking our way was a pick-up truck, upon which were welded metal boxes stuffed with hens and cockerels. This was Baltistan's equivalent of a mobile shop. It was surrounded by an animated crowd of local men accompanied by a gaggle of tiny children. The adults were poking and prodding the poultry to decide which ones were for the pot and which ones were to be kept for eggs. I ambled away to photograph the scene from afar when my attention was taken by an advancing crocodile of local children returning in their simple uniforms from school. Another roll of film bit the dust.

Back in the jeep, we followed the bank of the Indus towards Skardu. In the distance my eyes followed a series of black dots. As these specks moved nearer it dawned on me this must be a large herd of animals. I asked Jarputra to stop again and watched as the shapes began to take form. Out of the dusty cloud thundered a hundred or more black-and-white Nubian goats. To the side of them was a herdsman with two boys, urging the animals forward with their sticks. This farming life can have barely changed in a thousand years. It seemed almost sacrilege to film it.

We realized after a quick lunch why Jarputra had been so keen to drive us back to Skardu. A great honour had been bestowed on us – we were actually to open the specially arranged polo match and he was not only to drive us there but straight on to the pitch. Behind a football ground was a dusty rectangle with nothing more than two pairs of sticks indicating where the goals should be. One side was bordered by a disintegrating wall where hundreds of spectators sat. Sure enough, Jarputra drove onto the pitch sending clouds of dust over the assembled teams.

Polo is believed to have originated in Baltistan and it certainly seems to suit this nomadic, warlike race. Forget Windsor Great Park, Smith's Lawn or even the glamourous fictional world of polo created in Jilly Cooper's novel: rugged mountain horses are used instead of thoroughbreds, well-worn mufti replaces smart jodhpurs and shirts and team colours are just a basic red or white sash. One player did sport a badly fitting, if carefully brushed, riding hat but to avoid getting his prized possession marked he always put his hand or arm between the hat and the stick! I shook hands with the seven players in each team, wishing them well for the forthcoming battle as their mounts stamped impatiently. They all nodded but, as we spoke different languages, it was the symbolism that counted. The jeep was removed and, along with Baltistan's deputy commissioner, we were led to the grandstand and invited to sit on a carpeted terrace as a low enamel table piled with sweetmeats was placed in front of us. The whole area was shaded under a magnificent beech tree, known locally as the 'royal tree' since tradition decrees that no-one is allowed to take an axe to it.

Behind the deputy commissioner sat the chief of police. The two men wielded almost autonomous power in the region; only the army, who keep very much to themselves, are outside of their control. The deputy commissioner, about the same 5-feet 9-inch height as myself with piercing blue eyes and a neatly trimmed beard, had been born and raised in Skardu. Whenever I was to bump into him he was always smartly dressed, either in his official undyed linen shalwar qamis or in his smart Western clothes. The chief of police, by contrast, was a much more rugged type. He was a great bear of a man with rough, jet-black hair and a thick beard, reminding me of the pirate Cut-Throat Jake in the children's television cartoon, *Captain Pugwash*. Little could be seen of his face but a pair of dark eyes that gazed intently from beneath shaggy eyebrows. He was clearly a 'hands-on' man in his regalia of blue shirt, blue sweater, Sam Brown belt and sharply creased dark trousers tucked into highly polished calf-length black boots. Handing out business cards like some people cough, he informed me in deep sonorous tones that he was passionate about two things: polo and the lack of crime in the area. The latter was something he spoke about with great pride. His record sounded impressive, until you realized that people getting shot was still an everyday occurrence. However, this was classed simply as tribal disputes and not logged as crime at all. The main jail on the outskirts of Skardu has seen so little use there is a proposal to turn it into a theme hotel. I was a little dubious about the idea of a night behind bars in a Baltistan prison catching on as a holiday attraction in the West.

The police chief hit it off well with David who, also tall and bearded, was treated with respect by most of the Baltis who met him. However, our mild-mannered doctor left them baffled when he admitted that, after two years of marriage to Cath, he had no children. The chief of police proudly informed him that he had twelve. I was considered barely acceptable with two, but at least I had brought them along.

Polo as played in Baltistan appears to have no rules. I was asked whether they should play for an hour or until the first team reached nine goals. I opted for the former. Then I was presented with a hard white ball similar to, but slightly larger than, those used in cricket and apparently made up of sawdust and resin. I threw it high and hard. Both teams attacked, sticks clashing and mallet heads flying. The long mallets broke regularly and a chosen boy from each side stood at the bottom of our grandstand steps with his arms fulls of replacements. The player in need simply rode up at full speed, dropped the broken stick and adroitly snatched a new one in one fluid, non-stop motion. Being a spare-stick boy must be a bruising experience when the player's timing goes wrong. As the excitement level rose, the odd soft thud or crack would ring out as the rock-solid ball slammed into unprotected flesh or bone. This always led to aggressive retaliation and the game galloped along at a fierce pace. The dust kicked up by the ponies' flashing hooves made some of the intricate stick play impossible to see but, when frustration or simple bad temper got in the way of skill, it was hard to miss the players thwacking each other about the upper body or head with the shaft of their long mallets. Two balls were smashed to smithereens, so first Tom and then Kate was given the chance to start a new chukka. Each time they did so, a great roaring cheer went up from the crowd on the popular side and the cream of Skardu society around us applauded loudly. How proud Alison would have been to think of her daughter being the first female to start a rural polo match in northern Pakistan. Tom, Kate and I had plumped for the Crown Prince of Baltistan's red team and when they won by twelve goals to nine we were so caught up in it that we jumped up and shouted along with the rest of them.

That night at a dinner held for the children and me in the dining room at the K2 Motel Changez paid a moving tribute to Alison. Everywhere I went in this male-dominated country I was touched by the regard with which they held Alison and what she had stood for. Changez's warm voice was full of feeling: 'It is very rare in life when you have an occasion for remorse and celebration; unfortunately this is one of them. I am sorry for the death of your wife on K2 and we celebrate the fact that she climbed it. That is what she liked doing in life. She attained her ambition in the most dignified and noble manner. We feel for the children and for you. All of our hearts go out for you. We hope on your trek you are reminded of her in a way that is most befitting.'

The gathering expected me to say something. I searched for adequate words, climbed to my feet, took a deep breath and tried to convey some of the gratitude I felt for the overwhelming hospitality I had received. I also felt I owed them an explanation as to why I had travelled all this way with my two young children. 'It is a great privilege to have the support of the Pakistani Government and people for our journey from Scotland in the last few days. I don't know whether we will reach base camp; that is not what is important. The thing that is important is that when I had the saddest job of my life, to tell my children that their mother was dead, Tom said those few fateful words, 'Dad, please take me to see Mum's last mountain'. We flew from Islamabad to Skardu only a few days ago and it already seems a lifetime away because of the kindness and help we have received along the way. The pilots very kindly allowed us to share what must be the most beautiful commercial flight in the world. I and the two children were called forward just at the moment when K2 came on the horizon so the children were able to see the mountain. It was as if nature wanted us to see it, in perfect visibility in the most wonderful panorama of peaks. If nature wants to help us, and at the moment the weather is very settled and the rivers are very low, then in a short time they will be able to see K2 again, this time as their mother would have, from the ground, and that would not have been possible without the generosity, help and open-handedness of the Pakistani people.'

I sat down; there was little more I could add. Like Alison, I had been incredibly impressed by Skardu. It was nothing like the austere frontier town that I had been warned about. 'It's hard to get to and hard to get away from,' was the warning ringing in my ears as I left Britain. With weather like we had been seeing the pessimistic prophets could not have been more wrong.

Our final day was to be spent climbing up to the fortress that dominates the town from its hillside position on the side of the massive volcanic plug rising out of the flood plain. David and Cath opted instead to take up an invitation to see the local hospital. David told me later how they had been impressed with the standard of cleanliness and ratio of staff in the woman's ward, only to find when he went to the male area that the linen was dirty and the level of nursing staff poor. When he asked why this was, the doctor in charge explained, 'We thought you would only look in the women's ward'. However, they found most of the doctors well-trained, although there was a shortage of them. As in many parts of the world, Pakistani doctors seemed to prefer to remain in the cities rather than come to this cold frontier land. Staff were also keen to receive any spare medicines that David and Cath felt they could part with, so they promised to see what they could do on their return.

The rest of us set off in the jeeps but new concrete storm drains were being cast in the road and tree branches had been laid across it to prevent us going any further. We continued on foot, passing the oldest house in Skardu which, although the ground floor was a byre, was obviously still used as a home as we spotted a small boy peering from the tiny upper window. Spaces between the horizontal wooden blocks that had been used to construct it were filled with a mixture of sun-hardened mud and straw. How old it was no-one seemed to know.

The town came to an abrupt halt and the desert began. Soft, silk-smooth sand squelched underfoot as we passed bleached marble headstones in an old graveyard. The track up the cliff was steep, loose and narrow, which must have made it an uncompromising place to attack. The fort was built around 1840 to replace a much older construction that now lay in ruins, built by the founder of Baltistan, Ali Sher Khan. The lightly moustached prince, who I met at the polo match, was his direct descendant. This dynasty was still held in high regard by the local population, even though Baltistan was an integrated part of modern Pakistan. Another sign of what Changez described as the 'dichotomy' of life in the country, I supposed.

The wooden gates into the fort were so warped that we had to enter by squeezing through a tiny Judas gate to the side. I looked down through the battlements onto the Indus. It swirled around the foot of the rock over 150 metres (500 feet) below, where a man in a wooden boat pulled fishing nets against the currents. In the centre of the fort itself was a mosque, which purported to be the oldest in Pakistan. As we looked around these treasures, Tom and Kate entertained themselves by playing hide-and-seek. Only when dusk descended did we head back down the hillside.

Later that night Changez came to say farewell as we checked our tents on the lawn ready for what promised to be our first night's camp the following evening. We were to leave Skardu early next morning for a day's jeep ride to the start of our trek. He promised us fair weather for another four weeks. I wished I could share his confidence. He had been our link with the Pakistani Government, which had done everything in its power to help us on our way. All that this sociable man could add now was, 'Inshallah' – God willing.

CHAPTER SIX

THE WORST ROAD IN THE WORLD?

'One step forward, two steps back.'
VLADIMIR ILYICH LENIN

The small courtyard of the K2 Motel was designed when horses were the only form of transport, so our convoy of two pick-ups and two jeeps had a tight squeeze to fit in with all the other four-wheel drive vehicles now parked there. The luggage was loaded on to the largest pick-up, to be accompanied by our expedition organizer Ashraf, while the BBC and their equipment took up the other. Sudsy, Tom and I were in one jeep and Dave, Cath, Kate and Cally the other. The sky was blue and clear and the temperature in the high 80s (about 31 °C). The film crew, intending to shoot from the back of their open-topped pick-up, decided they needed scarves to wrap into turbans to keep the sun off their 'delicate complexions'. They headed off before us to stop at the bazaar to buy some suitable cloth. 'Give us fifteen minutes then set off. We should be in front of you,' commanded Chris Terrill as his team sped off. It was after 10.30 a.m. when we finally took to the road. Alison's diary reveals that her departure from the same place had been much earlier:

Friday 16 June. A great sleep. At 4.30 a.m. a knock on next door's window woke me. When my turn came I responded with an "OK". Straight up and into the shower. I wanted to wash my hair. I dried it then packed away the hairdryer – the last time it would be used for a few weeks. To breakfast, for omelette, coffee and toast. Around 5.30 a.m. we left in two jeeps full of people. I was in jeep two.

Just five minutes down the road we stopped at the petrol station. Within another half an hour we'd stopped again – this time due to a mechanical problem – and this carried on all day. Most of the jeeps seemed to have some sort of problem – either a flat tyre or a burst radiator. At many of the streams we stopped to get water for the radiators.

The road from Skardu headed down the bank of the Indus where three women were carrying conical willow baskets on their backs, each piled high with lavender. As we drove by the powerful aroma filled our jeeps. It was a fragrance we were to come across time and time again on our journey. Tom and Kate would roll the buds between their small fingers, bursting the fresh smell over all of us. Away from the town the desert returned with a vengeance; now only a modern suspension bridge separated us from the wide open spaces. This had been built by the military in the 1970s for access to the distant war zones and had replaced the old ferries that had plied the route for generations. Once over, the road turned from tarmac to compressed sand but in our four-by-fours we were able to progress steadily at around 25 mph. The sides of the road were marked by a trail of stones and beyond them stretched hundreds of miles of sand and scrub. We could see the track rolling off into the distance over the hilly terrain in front of us.

The scrub land could have been part of the Mohave Desert in America, which I had seen while climbing in the Joshua Tree National Park. Alison had been unable to exercise her rock skills on that trip because she was a month away from giving birth to Kate and found her second child was too low slung to do so comfortably. Instead, all she could do was sit with her feet up, appreciate the spectacular scenery and watch enviously...

Half-an-hour out of Skardu we hit our first police checkpoint. We had arranged permits for all the areas we were travelling through but I had no idea what had happened to them or who held our passports. By the time our jeep drew up at the road barrier, David, Cath, Cally and Kate and Ashraf in the luggage pick-up had arrived and had been waiting for a good ten minutes at the insistence of the armed sentry, who wanted me to sign for everyone before he would let the convoy pass. They were beginning to get grumpy in the heat and I could see I would get the blame. The policeman saluted me as I drove up, prompting David to nickname me 'the Grand Fromage'. I jumped out and strolled across to the official, who stood next to a low wooden bench under a small awning. Here I was handed the police book to sign. Ashraf had filled in all the relevant details except the parts about the passports and permits. Having neither, I simply signed my name with a flourish and handed the book back. The official did not even look at it – he had been forewarned about our visit and, once again, the red tape was cut to allow us on our way.

After our haphazard arrival at the police post Ashraf decided more decorum was needed. He ordered my jeep to go first with the other behind while he would follow on at the rear in the luggage truck. Much to our driver Jarputra's delight, we were now definitely 'number one' jeep, which sparked mock deference and much ribbing of me from the others. I could see I was going to be stuck with my sobriquet 'Grand Fromage' for the rest of the journey. The desert floor was littered with aromatic bushes releasing a wonderful herby bittersweet smell that wafted along with us as the road climbed in a series of hairpin bends towards a shady rock-lined pass. Below us was the original winding pathway, which had never been more than a cart-track. Our army-built road followed the path of the telegraph poles that linked the next town of Shigar with the outside world.

Collections of red iron-tinged boulders dotted the beige landscape and every so often these would be joined by a maze of dry-stone walls, originally designed to keep stock in, although as they had been worn down over the years large gaps had appeared. They would occasionally provide shelter for the odd exposed herdsman's hut, the most substantial of which had only simple walls of slatted wooden hurdles and crude roofing made out of bundles of dried grass. In summer they would provide some welcome shade from the unremitting sun but must be little help in the driving rain and snow of winter.

The land dropped away and we realized we had been driving along a high plateau. Below us we had clear views of the Shigar river, although it required a metaphorical rubbing of the eyes to convince ourselves the stunning panorama was not a mirage. On the right flank, the hillside looked like nothing more than arid desert, but this was cut by the wide, mirror-smooth river that meandered lazily across the valley, bringing with it every drop of snow or ice that melts on K2. What really drew our eyes, however, was the verdant green of Shigar itself. The natural springs of clean, reliable water had allowed the cluster of houses to establish a profitable and successful agricultural living growing cereals and fruits, which provided a feast of colours on this table of sand. Beyond it was the Haramosh range. We had seen one end of these mountains in Skardu; now we were looking at it side-on. Peak after peak bobbed on the skyline like choppy waves in a brown sea, dark except for the occasional glinting field of ice. It looked like wild, exciting country and I vowed to return to explore more of it as soon as I got the chance.

We had been driving for over an hour, the outskirts of Shigar were in sight but there was still no sign of the BBC. I knew they tried to be inconspicuous but this was getting beyond a joke. After discussion with the rest of the team we decided they must still be behind us and stopped the jeeps at a scattering of houses to wait. Here children worked in the field and hens, goats and sheep gathered around a small watering-hole. Tom and Kate held hands with David and Cath who wanted to take some photographs as I slipped down an inviting tunnel between the little square houses to find strings of shiny red chillies drying in the sunshine. After shooting off a few frames, I slowly made my way back to the jeeps to find the BBC crew had finally caught up with us. Chris Terrill, done up like Lawrence of Arabia with a long colourful scarf wrapped round his head and shoulders, was standing waving angrily in the back of his jeep. We had accidentally passed them on the outskirts of Skardu and they were not happy. It was back up the road a couple of miles for all of us to allow them to get some film of us in the desert.

It was after 1.00 p.m. when we arrived at the Shigar government rest house where we had been due for morning tea at 10.30 a.m., as the waiting inspector of police informed us sternly. Naturally, I blamed the BBC, and he nodded sagely in agreement, assuming our film crew would be 'artistic' types who had to be humoured. Government rest houses were built in colonial days as a place for civil servants to stay while on official business. Providing sitting room, bedrooms, bathrooms, cook and caretaker, all you had to do was bring your own food for the length of your stay. These rest houses are dotted all over Pakistan and the Indian subcontinent and are situated so as to be no more than a day's horse ride away from each other.

Chairs and low tables had been set out in an oval on the main lawn. These were laden with plates of assorted sticky biscuits and a selection of overcooked chicken bits that had clearly been sitting in the sun for a considerable time. As we were running late most of the local dignitaries who had gathered for the obligatory tea ceremony had dispersed, obviously fed up with waiting. Instead, we found a party of English ladies dressed in linen suits and flowery dresses, who informed me they were on a three-week 'adventure safari'. We were at 2240 metres (7350 feet) but could have been at a garden party on the south coast of England.

'I am from Brighton and have been here for a fortnight,' said a white-haired woman wearing a wide floppy hat, cotton blouse and long patterned skirt. 'We are not going to Askoli like yourselves – this is as far as we go – nothing as strenuous as your expedition but it is fantastic anyway.' I was tempted to ask her age, remembering the criticism levelled at me for bringing children to this area. 'I am seventy-five,' she answered proudly. 'Anyone could come here if they wanted. If they feel they can, they can.'

Encouraged by her defiant spirit I downed my tea and we all clambered on board our jeeps once more to head down through the shade and greenery of Shigar itself. The main street was made up of the now familiar wooden Tibetan-style houses with their distinctive overhanging balconies but the road was so narrow we had to take a detour. Our path wound down between more basic flat-roofed houses with low doorways and tiny slits for windows. Rustic handmade ladders were propped against the walls leading to the roof where makeshift woven partitions made open-air room dividers so families could move up there in the better weather. In these back streets we saw more of the elusive women, most of whom were veiled in bright red, orange and pink material. Demure but curious, they crept forward behind the mud-and-straw walls with their covered heads bowed until, at the last moment, they popped up with a cheeky grin and dared you to take their picture. If you were a second slow with the shutter release they were gone.

At this point the BBC realised one of their walkie-talkies had gone missing. As I had it last I was not popular and knew I must have mislaid it back in the desert. Things were not helped by the fact that we were running late for our next appointment, so there was a slight tetchiness in the air as we left the village and took to the open road once more. The track beneath us was again compressed sand so we accelerated smoothly and put a few miles under our belt. Tongol, at the end of this jeep road and where we were to make our first camp, was over seven hours away and that was without our obligatory stops to meet the local dignitaries at each hamlet. I began to feel a slight apprehension that it would be dark by the time we finally arrived at our destination. By now we should have been having lunch in the village of Dasso, where the valley turns sharply east up the Braldo river, and we were less than halfway there. There was nothing for it but sit back and let the journey unfold. Alison's diary recounts a similar experience of the jeep road:

> *Friday 16 June. Picnic under the shade of trees at noon. Dusty but great fun. This morning we had a tea-and-biscuit stop at a village that consisted of a couple of houses. What a strange, rough yet easy world. We bounce up and down in the dust and heat for seven hours and then get waited on hand and foot.*

We passed by a white outcrop where two men were swinging a pair of sledgehammers and I was informed by an ever-helpful Jarputra that this was the local marble factory. The jeeps hugged the Shigar river, across which we could see the jagged crests of the Haramosh range. They made the Chamonix Aiguille in France look like stepping stones. As I surveyed the mountainsides my imagination soared to the climbing possibilities they would offer. Grey-white glaciers poked their snouts from between these superb peaks; some of the icy fingers joined up and forced their way down the valley sides like a giant hand before narrowing again as they ground into the lower ravines that led down to the river. At the end of these gullies, just at the point where the melting ice poured into the river, was a smattering of green as small cultivated hamlets of one or two houses made the most of the pure water supply. I pointed this out to Tom, feeling few things could help his education and understanding of the natural world more than seeing such sights for real.

On our side of the river, immediately above us, was the barren Mango range. Across these desert mountains is the most direct route to Askoli, the hamlet at the end of the valley into K2, but this route can only be done on foot and is at least seven days walk through passes that reach 5070 metres (16 000 feet). Even my two hyperactive offspring would have been hard-pushed to do that as a preliminary to the rest of the trek. The advent of the jeep roads up the Shigar and then Braldo river valleys have dramatically improved accessibility to the Karakoram. Most climbers and trekkers can now reach the remote outpost of Askoli under diesel power before beginning their walk to K2 and the other major peaks.

I had been recording my thoughts and observations on tape while Tom stood between my legs and listened. Every so often he would be inspired to take the tape recorder from me to add his own comments. 'It is nice here, there are lots of big rivers and it is fun riding in a jeep, although it might be better on a motorbike because there are lots of huge big holes,' he recounted formally at this point. At little later he added, 'There are lots of rocks, some in the river and some are on the road. I can see a windsock in front and lots of guards. I think this is a war place.'

He was right. In the far distance was an army road block but as we approached it a commotion broke out behind us. Lights flashed and horns honked – something was clearly amiss so we pulled up, expecting it to be Chris Terrill, aka Lawrence of Arabia, wanting to make some directorial changes. But no. Two dark Toyota Land Cruisers with blue lights on top raced up behind us. Four or five armed police stepped out and crunched across the sand in smartly polished black boots with toe caps a drill sergeant would be proud of, forming a line in front of me. Down it walked the deputy commissioner I had met at the polo match in Skardu. In diamond-checked Jacquard pullover and Ray Bans he looked distinctly out of place in this wild spot. 'Ah Mr Ballard, it is so nice to see you again,' he said warmly. I relaxed. We shook hands, his dry ones clasping my slightly sweaty palms. 'We heard you had been delayed and thought we had better check nothing was wrong. Please come and have some tea.' He pointed towards the checkpoint, his dark glasses glinting in the sun. Another familiar figure appeared, his swagger stick at a jaunty angle – it was the stocky black-bearded chief of police. These two high rollers jumped back into their four-by-fours and sped away in front of us in a cloud of dust, drawing to a sharp halt at the road block. We followed in a slower convoy. Tea, with the usual accompanying delicacies – biscuits, cakes, fried chicken – was set out on a makeshift veranda in front of the army post. I wondered how they had managed to rustle up such a feast in this windswept and desolate spot.

As I sat down on a pile of silk cushions next to the deputy commissioner he explained that this was the first time he had made the journey up this particular valley. We talked about the orchards of apricots I had seen earlier and he reminded me of the Baltistani belief that the fruit can help with acclimatization. The army officer in charge could not speak English but must have understood a little of what we were talking about as he rose and came back a few moments later with a huge pack of army-issue dried apricots. He popped one in his mouth so I followed his example. The texture was of hardened chewing gum but, when I rolled it round my mouth, the flavour burst through suddenly in a delcious tangy punch. I washed it down with hot sweet tea, made this time from black leaves and evaporated milk – what my old father in his army days would have called 'gunfire'.

When it was time to leave we were given a police escort as far as Dasso. The sandy track became more corrugated and as we hopped along the regular cry of 'ouch!' came from the BBC team, who had squeezed into the back of our vehicle to film. Chris Terrill, taller than the rest of us and cramped into the luggage space, was finding it difficult to stop his turbaned head bouncing off the jeep roof. The scrub desert and bleak terrain continued until we turned a sharp bend and found ourselves in front of the Dasso bridge. In the old days this was where most expeditions foundered. Then, the river could only be crossed using rickety ferry boats and that was only when the river level was low enough. Our police escort stopped and drew aside to give us the dubious privilege of being the first across the suspension bridge, which was 30 metres or so (about 100 feet) wide. Several large planks from the carriageway were missing after floods and through the gaping holes we could see the swollen rushing waters. It was a jolting and nervous struggle to the far bank. Once over and around the corner we found Dasso and another government rest house. We were over two hours late and, as it was a Friday, the rabbit hutch-like shops were closed, but the crowds were still waiting for us. Another round of hand-shaking had to be made before we could escape inside for lunch. Ashraf sped into action unloading the white cardboard lunch boxes he had brought along from the K2 Motel. The friendly manager had thoughtfully tied the vegetarian ones with a green ribbon. Inside were hard-boiled eggs, cheese spread, biscuits, apples and grapes, with cold lemon juice to wash it all down.

It was after 3.00 p.m. by the time we left and we had been warned it would start to get dark around 5.00 p.m. We were barely halfway into our day's journey and the track we were soon creeping along made the previous sections seem like a billiard table by comparison. Between Dasso and Tongol the road needs to be continually rebuilt or dug out as the combination of fluctuating river levels and landslides often leaves it unstable and impassable. The track would alternate between hugging the river and traversing the hillside up above it. It was a masterpiece of route-finding.

We had gone only a few miles when we hit our first spot of trouble. Storms had simply washed away a huge section of the road, leaving it only just wide enough to pass. I felt mildly uncomfortable next to Jarputra hugging the wall but I could see Sudsy, sitting behind him and looking straight down into the river as the wheels only just gripped the bank, going pale. 'You are lucky the river is so low at the moment,' piped up Jarputra cheerfully, pulling his offside mirror in so it would not scratch against the rock side. We crossed another, more solid, suspension bridge and were back on the right bank. The pebble track turned to sand again, supported only by a hand-built dry-stone wall, as we began to climb a series of shoulders and zigzagged steeply upwards. 'It's very dramatic,' Sudsy shouted breathlessly.

'I didn't think Sutherlands had the word "dramatic" in his vocabulary,' I countered, but understood exactly how he felt. Tom, loving every minute of this adventure and oblivious to the real dangers, chose this moment to pick up the tape recorder. 'This is a very exciting drive but it is very nice.' His exhilarated child's voice could only just be heard about the roar of the river and the crunch of the gears. 'We have to drive very carefully because we are so close to the water and the mountains, which have lots of landslides.' Chris Terrill had his BBC boys swing out as wide as possible to get the best shots as the rest of us wound on uphill, the back wheels of the pick-up virtually hanging off the crumbling ledge.

A huge landslide had buried the original line of the track. The new road zigzagged down this debris of rock and sludge and the drivers had to ease the vehicles slowly over the unpredictable scree. The hillside was still moving and you could see the sand and gravel sliding softly towards the river. All our thoughts were on getting through this without ending up in the water. Everyone, that is, except our fearless BBC team; Chris Terrill and his crew continued to film as we negotiated even the most treacherous bends.

The road evened out and the rest of us drove on a short distance as the BBC sorted out some technical details. We stopped under some water-polished pockmarked slabs to wait for them. This was too much for the rock climber in me and I could not resist an attempt at the obvious crackline. As I scrambled up Tom followed closely behind until he got dangerously high and I sent him back down sternly. Cunning Kate, who had slipped out of the second jeep, had gone for a more careful horizontal traverse in her bare feet and, although she got no higher than head height, clearly enjoyed the physical challenge.

Dusk made the road even more difficult to make out. We had reached the crest of a long ascent when, just as we were about to make a sharp bend and start our way down a series of twisting bends, we were met by a pair of headlights. It was the local supply jeep. The driver looked at us blankly. There was no way he could reverse. Jarputra shouted back to the other drivers. They were going to have to take on this difficult job. To one side of us was a 300-foot drop down to the river. Suds and I looked at each other and without a word picked up Tom and climbed out. The road was not wide enough to get a foothold beside the jeep so we had to steady ourselves on the scree slope below it. The vehicles moved backwards inch by inch. A cry of horror went up from the rest of the ashen-faced team, who had only now cottoned on to what was happening. It was too late. They had to sit there as the jeeps made the slow reverse journey for half a mile. One wrong movement and the wheels would have slipped off into space. The supply truck followed them down as Suds, Tom and I clambered on to the road and walked on to wait for the procedure to be over.

Our way was now lit only by the two big circles coming from our headlights. Tom, wide awake and excited, grasped the tape recorder. 'We have gone past some stone huts. Dad thinks people live in those huts. The river is very rough. This is a new road but the old road has been washed away by the rain and rocks.'

Hugging the vertical cliffs were piles of mud, sand and boulders that masqueraded as a road. It looked about the width of an average Western footpath. The headlights reflected off the smooth rock walls to our right. Sweat poured from beneath Jarputra's woollen nating. 'Sir, Mr James, this is a very dangerous place,' he said between clenched teeth. Suds coughed gently from the back. He had once been a minder to the Princess Royal's boys in the Scottish mountains in winter – a breeze compared with this.

Before us was another wooden suspension bridge. We had to cross it. Tom was thrilled. He leaned out of the side window – I had opened all of them, figuring that if we going in the water at least I would be able to get Tom by the scruff of the neck and have a fighting chance of swimming our way out. The jeep swung on to the rocking bridge. I peered out straight into the glacial meltwater rushing below us. Tom assumed we were all quiet because we wanted to savour the moment; he did not recognize our terror. We felt the wooden planks buckle and bow beneath us. The white foam from the torrent below loomed closer than ever. Then we were over and back on firm ground.

The track hugged the bank and we jolted up the hillside through magnificent looming rocks that appeared as ghostly shapes in the headlights' beams. We started another big climb. Were we really going up and across that steep slanting gully? We stopped. Suds wondered out loud if we should get out and walk again. Tom stood up to get a better view. I was sure even Jarputra, our fearless Hunza, looked pale. The jeep dropped into low gear, he slammed his foot down hard on the accelerator and the dry gravel beneath us crackled. We were committed. The jeep thundered up the steep scree incline. The crest was in sight. Suddenly we were over, past a few shepherd huts and hurtling along a straight but deeply rutted sandy stretch. The drop back down to the river looked impossible: the bends were too tight and there was no way the jeeps and pick-ups could make them in one go. Jarputra had to stop, engage reverse, hold the jeep on its hand brake and then go forward again. This had to be repeated two or three times until we were round and rattling forward to the next one to repeat the manoeuvre all over again.

Some lights appeared ahead. We breathed a sigh of relief: could this be Tongol, where we were to spend the night? No, we were still

ABOVE: A promise made, a promise kept. K2 dominates the horizon from the cockpit window on the flight to Skardu. *(PHOTOGRAPH BY JAMES BALLARD)*

BELOW: It's better to travel than arrive. Jim and Kate on the jeep journey.

(PHOTOGRAPH BY CATH COLLIER)

*Yet another tea ceremony
with the deputy commissioner
and chief of police.*
(PHOTOGRAPH BY DAVID COLLIER)

*Jim above where the river
and desert meet.*
(PHOTOGRAPH BY DAVID COLLIER)

ABOVE: Gateway to the Baltoro. *(PHOTOGRAPH BY JAMES BALLARD)*
BELOW: Kate with her two minders, Ibrahim and Tom, on the road to Askoli.
(PHOTOGRAPH BY JAMES BALLARD)

Girls just want to have fun...
Cally and Cath on the Flying
Fox bridge.
<small>(PHOTOGRAPH BY JAMES BALLARD)</small>

... and boys too. Ian 'Suds'
Sutherland on his way
across.
<small>(PHOTOGRAPH BY DAVID COLLIER)</small>

ABOVE: *Tom and Kate at school in the Karakoram with Cally.* (PHOTOGRAPH BY JAMES BALLARD)
BELOW: *Following the leader.* (PHOTOGRAPH BY JAMES BALLARD)

'Why didn't you bring the Lego, Dad?' (Tom and Kate on the Baltoro)

(PHOTOGRAPH BY CALLY FLEMING)

Harvest time Baltistan-style.

(PHOTOGRAPH BY JAMES BALLARD)

Tom and Brown Bear's drawing for Mum.
(PHOTOGRAPH BY JAMES BALLARD)

A rare lie-in for Tom and Kate.
(PHOTOGRAPH BY JAMES BALLARD)

Mountains of splendour.
(PHOTOGRAPH BY DAVID COLLIER)

Tom, Kate and Jim
visit Pakistan's monument
to Alison.
(PHOTOGRAPH BY DAVID COLLIER)

not there, it was Hoto. We pulled into a government rest house and found the deputy commissioner and chief of police waiting for us again. They offered us a spot of tea which we declined gracefully and were soon back on the road. We were keen to end this nightmare stretch as soon as possible. It seemed an age bumping through the blackness as the route alternated between precarious hairpin bends and long straight stretches. Jarputra seemed more relaxed. He must have known the worst was over. I asked him if it was. 'I don't know Mr James, I have never been along this route before.' I was glad I had not quizzed him earlier.

We rounded one last shoulder and there in front of us were the distant lights of Tongol. We were over three hours late but the whole population and those from the surrounding hamlets of Sino, Surungo and Askoli appeared to be waiting for us. A huge banner had been stretched across the road between two tall trees and a cheer rose up as our dusty convoy drove through. Never before had I so looked forward to a welcome ceremony and its copious cups of tea.

CHAPTER SEVEN

ACCLIMATIZATION

'So many worlds, so much to do,
So little done, such things to be.'
ALFRED LORD TENNYSON

The jeeps' headlights cast their long beams over three low stone buildings as we pulled on to a gentle slope and stopped. This was as far as we could go on four wheels. Normally the road runs on to Askoli but floods had washed away the last 3 miles or so of track. There was a muffled scuffling as the large welcome party moved round to get a better view of us. Our strange convoy seemed to hold more-than-usual fascination for the remote village dwellers, who continued to linger long after the usual formalities were over. Through the darkness our eyes began to make out a flickering light. We headed in that direction, realizing it must be the mess tent Ashraf had promised, as he had sent an advance party to set up the cooking facilities. A paraffin lamp threw an orange glow over the cosy scene underneath the canvas, where inviting chairs had been laid out around a long rectangular table set for dinner. Ashraf informed me food was ready whenever we wanted it and hot drinks were already being handed round. I gulped one down but decided we should put up our tents before anything else. Leaving a well wrapped-up Tom and Kate – the temperatures were plummeting by now – in the capable hands of Cally and Cath, I went to inspect the site.

We had six tents to erect altogether: the large family tent for Tom, Kate and me and five others for the film crew and the rest of the team. Suds, David and I climbed onto the back of the baggage truck for a bumpy ride over the adjoining fields to the camping area. We unloaded and got down to work in absolute blackness with only the pale beams from our head torches to light our way. We were using freestanding mountain tents, ideal because we could put them up and then move them into position before pegging them to the ground at an appropriate spot. I had spent my twelfth birthday under canvas and plenty of nights in the intervening thirty-seven years since, so with the experienced help of Suds and David it did not take us long. In under an hour we had finished and were ready for a very welcome supper.

The BBC crew had lined up the plastic barrels around the mess tent and upon one of them had been placed an aluminium bowl of hot water, a cake of soap and a clean towel so that everyone could wash their hands. The entrance flaps had been brought down to keep it warm for a sleepy Tom and Kate and, by the time we all gathered around the table, it was nicely protected against the now-icy temperature outside. Ashraf's personal team had been frying and boiling away in the kitchen hours before our arrival and no sooner were we seated than a huge tureen of tomato soup was placed in front of us alongside a pile of delicious fresh nans. Most of us were too tired and hungry to talk, but every so often a particularly treacherous moment on our recent jeep ride would come back to us – we could laugh about it now. Great trays of roast chicken and chips or pasta with vegetable sauce were brought out and we tucked in greedily. Sudsy rounded it off by breaking out a round of Mars bars from our luxury rations. He was supposed to be the only one who knew where everything was but within twenty-four hours he had noticed the lid on this particular barrel was not clicked back into place. He did not have to be Sherlock Holmes to track down a small boy with a ring of chocolate around his mouth. I was secretly impressed that Tom had managed to deduce where this treasure-trove of food was and had worked out how the locking mechanisms opened. However, his actions were not in the team spirit and I pulled him aside and gave him a severe reprimand, pointing out he must always see Suds and ask permission before going into the barrels for anything, particularly food that might be needed later.

The meal over, I got the children ready for bed, Ashraf having delivered more hot clean water for washing and teeth-cleaning. Tom climbed into the tent first and undressed before clambering into his sleeping bag where a hot-water bottle and Brown Bear were waiting for him. I helped Kate lay her clothes out for the morning and then slid her into the next sleeping bag along. I walked away for a few moments to give them a chance to settle down, only to find them fast asleep upon my return. I left the front flap open as I got into the sleeping bag nearest the door. There was something deliciously primitive about climbing into this womb-like warmth after a long hard day and being able to lie there looking at the stars. Three months earlier, Alison would have been gazing up at a similar night sky. Her diary entry for that time read:

> *Friday 16 June, Askoli. As we step out of our jeeps the mess and kitchen tents go up. Stoves are produced, and within a few minutes we are served hot tea. By now we have already been shown places to go and lie and rest...Dinner is finally ready at around 7.00 p.m. — soup, chicken and chips (third time so far!) and jelly. Tomorrow we expect to be very hot and so are being woken at 4.30 a.m. to start the trek around 5.30 a.m. Bed 8.30 p.m.*

For Tom and Kate, camping was second nature; they had been doing it ever since they were born. We had spent an enormous amount of time as a family living under canvas — it was only in the past year that Alison's climbing demands had taken her away on her own. In 1994, when we all went to Everest base camp, our 2-metre-square tent became our home for three months and, although Alison spent periods on the mountain, the rest of her time at base camp was with the children. We developed a way of sleeping in these wild places that we called the 'sandwich technique'. Alison and I would take opposite ends so that the children always knew whichever way they turned either Mum or Dad would be there if they woke up in the night. We found that Kate would always gravitate to my side no matter where she started off and Tom would always end up by his mother's side. Now that Alison was no longer there, Tom had to take a more responsible big-brother role and became the new back stop for Kate. Living such an intimate existence inevitably brings you close as a family but it did not mean we could not have our own space when we wanted it. Alison or I could easily take a break and although a young child can't go off on its own we allowed our two considerable freedom by letting them dig a dam in a stream or play on a beach and just kept an eye on them from a distance.

It was really quite a mundane life and one that helped keep Alison's feet planted firmly in reality when the rest of her life was taken up with ever-greater mountaineering challenges. When she came down from a climb she liked nothing better than to wade streams, scramble up trees and romp with Tom and Kate. When we were camping in Europe in 1993 she soloed a brand-new route on the Eiger and then stumbled across a dead climber on the way down, which left her in tears. She then had to go through all the Swiss red tape to get the body out and travel on the same train as the dead man's partner, only to find when she got back to the camp site that all Kate wanted was a swing. Her return from the north face of the Matterhorn was greeted with enthusiastic cries from Tom and Kate, not for her achievement but because they wanted to drag her round the toy shops. When she had completed the Shroud on the Grande Jorasses she came back exhausted in the twilight to find the children asleep and oblivious to their mother's record-breaking climb...

I woke just after 6.00 a.m. as the sun was beginning to paint the first orange streaks on the peaks in front of us. It was yet another clear, cold morning. Tom and Kate slept on as I climbed out to find Suds and David already standing chatting in their duvet jackets outside the mess tent. As I reached them an arm popped out from beneath the canvas and placed a large mug of hot sweet tea in my hand. I enjoyed a few minutes of tranquillity before I heard Kate's piercing cry, 'Daaad, Daaad, I want a wee'. The peace was shattered for another day. I swilled down the last dregs and made my way back across to a tousle-haired Kate, who was sitting up in her sleeping bag. I picked her up and carried her in the direction of the toilet block which, I had been told, was somewhere near the river at the bottom end of our field. We passed the low thatched buildings, a dirty-looking shack and, below the track, a solitary small stone dwelling with a little veranda, upon which four or five local men were crouched making a hot drink. I felt their curious eyes follow me and my chattering curly-haired bundle, and shouted a greeting to them. 'Morning Sir,' they replied politely before returning to their own quiet murmurs. The toilet was nothing more than three stone stalls with a hole to squat in, but at least it looked clean and was as good as anything we were to find later. As we returned Kate spotted Cath in her tent having a cup of tea and ran over with her usual, 'Caff, Caff, I want a cuddle'. Tom had stirred and was getting dressed so I put the sleeping bags out to air and we made our way over to the mess tent to see what was for breakfast. As the tables were being laid Ashraf introduced us to his kitchen crew of strapping, typically tall Hushe men: Ibrahim, who helped around the kitchen and had also been delegated to act as Kate's personal minder; the cook, his cousin 'Little' Ibrahim (over 6 feet tall); Abdul, the assistant cook and Ashraf's assistant, Saleem. The rest of the porters were to be hired locally before we set off in a couple of days.

Breakfast consisted of warm chapattis presented in a pancake-like pile, cornflakes, tea, hot water for coffee, fried or scrambled eggs and jam. We were at 2930 metres (9600 feet) but no-one was feeling the affects of altitude except that we all seemed to have ravenous appetites. Abdul came round with a large jug and asked, 'miluk?' Tom and Kate, who quickly grasped he was asking them if they wanted milk for their cereal, thought this pronunciation hilarious and adopted it as their own. As we tucked in I began to realise what a goldfish must feel like because all the locals from Tongol and the surrounding villages had once again drifted down to our site and stood in a line looking in at us curiously.

Cath decided it was time for Tom to get down to some work. She led him to a secluded spot and out came the school books. No sooner had they set out their makeshift classroom than the local children started to gather round. They didn't make a sound but arrived in dribs and drabs, watching from behind some low bushes as Tom did his sums and reading. Poor Tom just tried to ignore them by putting his head down and focusing on the work in front of him. It had been well drummed into him before he left that he must keep up his schoolwork while we were away. Luckily Cath's unorthodox and entertaining teaching methods meant he was almost reluctant to shut his book when she had to finish for the day.

We had been warned to expect the chief of police and deputy commissioner for morning tea and, sure enough, shortly after 10.30 a.m. we spotted the blue flashing lights and dusty convoy making their way along the last straight stretch of the road into Tongol. The usual round of handshakes followed, then down to the police post for tea. They informed me that we had been invited to meet the mayor of Askoli and they would walk there with us before lunch.

Cally and David were both feeling slightly under par so they remained in camp as the rest of our little party set off up the path. Tom was on foot like the rest of us, while Kate perched proudly on the back of Ibrahim. This 6-feet 6-inch Hushe giant was a specialist high-altitude porter, having summited Chogolisa (7654 metres/25 000 feet) and Gasherbrum II (8035 metres/26 360 feet) and been up to 7600 metres (24 800 feet) on K2 a couple of times. A more experienced porter would have been hard to find and, as Ashraf's most trusted employee, he was given the most valuable load. Ibrahim took his role very seriously and strutted up the path with his Kate-filled papoose squirming contentedly on his back. On the days we trekked she would sleep, eat and laugh from her elevated seat, completely at ease with this huge man. Although they did not speak a word of the same language they would chat away for hours and seemed to understand each other. Even when Kate ran around on her own, Ibrahim's black eyes would follow her every move protectively.

Around us the jagged snow-topped mountains looked like high alpine scenery, magnified many times over. The hamlets of Tongol,

Surungo and Askoli lie on a rocky shelf cut off from the riverbank by coarse pudding stone cliffs that are pummelled into a new shape every time a flash flood or prolonged storm hits the area. Every so often we would come across a handful of local people who appeared to have come down just to have a look at us before returning to their cereal fields. We passed alongside crops of buckwheat in the early stages of being harvested. Among the workers was a bent old man with a face like a prune who was hacking slowly at the crops with a small, saw-edged sickle, slicing off the stalks in handfuls and laying them in a spiral pattern to air. It seemed extremely arduous work, especially for someone who looked about eighty-five years old. When we approached, we were shocked to hear him say he was just thirty-five. Sudsy was particularly fascinated, as his grandmother had worked a croft in Scotland and he had grown up watching much the same harvesting techniques. A child's small filthy hand proffered a sickle and our safety officer took up the challenge eagerly. He brought it across with an aggressive swish; the buckwheat bent but the blunt instrument simply slid away. He tried again, with little more success. Our tough mountain rescuer handed the implement back sheepishly to a six-year-old-girl, who took up the back-breaking work with practised dexterity. Women were sitting on the dusty earth gleaning what was left, their angular faces prematurely aged by the harsh sun and savage cold of their mountain existence. Working the next field alone was a mother and her four children. They wanted to talk but would not be photographed, shying away aghast as soon as the lens was pointed in their direction. We chatted away, neither understanding the other but conveying what we wanted by hand signals and wild gesticulations.

The entire middle section of the main jeep road to Askoli had been washed away, so we had to follow a higher footpath. The road will be rebuilt in time for the trekkers next year but in the meantime locals are left with a very sketchy path. It wound alongside the cliff, rising to over 30 metres (100 feet) as the route narrowed to barely more than a few inches. We hugged the rock side as we inched along, fearing the remaining ground underfoot might start to drop away.

Ibrahim strolled off into the distance as if he and Kate were just going for some groceries down Fort William high street. Tom, with adjustable ski poles to help him keep his balance, was sandwiched between myself and Suds so we could grab him if the track disintegrated. The path was just one step inside the line between danger and adventure – a line that I had promised I would not cross on this trip with my children. We tiptoed onwards and within an hour were scrambling up the first fields of Askoli.

We found the mayor's short, slight figure waiting for us as we came up the hill. I shook his leather-gloved right hand – he explained he wore it on one hand only for the cold. When the valley was a military-restricted zone the Government had insisted expeditions bought their supplies in Askoli and before the jeep road was extended past Dasso all trekkers used Askoli as a stopping-off point. Traditionally, the last day of civilization would involve a walk from Chango, just across the river from the village of Hoto, to Askoli, where climbers would stock up on local produce. Chango was eventually destroyed by a rock avalanche. Then, a few years ago, the military lifted restrictions in the area and extended the jeep road. The population of Askoli seemed to have picked up all the bad vices of our Western culture. It was also extremely dirty and Cath became indignant that the mayor (really more of a tribal headman), who lived in relative luxury, had let it fall into such a state. The village's reputation is so unpleasant that these days most people simply pass on through. Some of the village boys unsettled Tom by running up close and leering rudely at him. They were around the same size as him but their rugged, lived-in faces revealed their true age to be somewhere in their teens. All Tom could do was glare back angrily but, being vastly outnumbered, he stayed close between Sudsy and me.

Our party was led into a small, squat building, similar to every other one in the village. We squeezed into the main living area, which was as black as Old Nick's waistcoat and full of swirling smoke. A large square hole in the front of the mud roof acted as a chimney. Unfortunately, the open fire was at the far end of the room and the billowing fumes stung the eyes and clawed suffocatingly at the back of the throat. Hot water boiled in a pan sitting on three soot-blackened stones placed around the hearth. Tea was to be served in the bedroom, which, I understood, doubled as the mayoral chambers. The mayor's tired-looking wife was dispatched to fetch more dry wood so that this upper floor could be heated. I watched her stumble outside and return a few moments later with a handful of logs. Laying them quietly on the earthen floor in the corner she then proceeded to split them with a battered old adze. Two younger girls sat with us. Balti tradition allows men to have up to four wives and I wondered if these girls were other, more recent, brides. Their bright darting eyes and clawing hands were eager for anything we could give them, particularly money. After seeing so many of these traditional wood and daub houses along our route, I was fascinated to see one from the inside. In the depths of winter the inhabitants move into the crudely dug-out cellar with their animals to escape the worst of the cold. In better weather they can use the main living space and then, in the heat of the summer, move on to the roof.

Tea was finally called, so we all trooped back into the house and were pointed up a thin trellis-like ladder. Bits of wood had been crudely slashed together with great gaps between the rungs in some parts. Needless to say, we trod with great care. Upstairs, we found ourselves on a Tibetan-style balcony, although the once-ornate wooden carved panels had obviously seen better days. I had to bend double to get through the low door leading from there into the bedroom, where a striped nylon garden chair at the head of an aluminium picnic table was pulled out for me to sit in. My shoes sank into luxurious pile. I glanced down and saw a fabulous handmade carpet spread out over the dusty floor. The thin china cups set before us were clean, or at least looked it, although Cath gave me a worried look as Tom and Kate put them to their lips. The tea, for which we had reassuringly seen the boiling water, was aromatic and slipped down well as we chatted politely to our host. His few words of broken English were expanded upon by his son, who spoke more fluently.

Our cups were continually refilled until we eventually took our leave and, thanking our hosts, set off to make the precarious hike back to camp. Swatting away the more persistent children we walked slowly to defend a tired Tom.

Supper was a relaxed affair and afterwards, in the flickering light of the paraffin lamp, Ashraf's kitchen team pulled out the 'drums' — which looked distinctly like the aluminium cooking pots we had seen our dinner made in earlier. The slow, heavy beat began to pick up, toes started to tap and before long the tall Hushe men were kicking up the dust as they swung their bodies to the powerful rhythm. We sat on the ground or on logs and barrels and clapped along until Tom and Kate started to nod off and I carried them to bed.

As a young boy I had marvelled at old black-and-white photographs of the early explorers soaking in sulphur baths. Askoli, the name of the place where they had been found, had always remained with me, but when I mentioned them to the deputy commissioner he looked at me blankly and said he knew of none near the village. I scoured the maps along our route and finally found a small reference to them. They were just a few hours walk from Tongol and I decided we should use our last day in the hamlet to visit the spot. Ibrahim, with Kate tucked safely on his back, led the way up the mean gully that cut through the pudding stone cliffs we had seen the day before. Various ancient larva flows led us round volcanic rock formations into a bizarre-looking moonscape and here in two murky pools were the rich sulphur waters. The steaming rocks were lined with slippery green algae and hairy plant growth and the sulphur left a mild eggy smell in the air. The water temperature felt like a very hot domestic bath and we all took turns to ease our limbs into the mellow warmth. They reminded me of the 'slipper baths' I used to find at public swimming pools in Sheffield when I was a boy. These small tiled tubs would be regularly topped up by enormous brass taps, leaving them steaming hot. One was supposed to use them to wash before entering the main pool but us youngsters liked nothing better than to lie soaking in their heat for hours. In the sulphur pools the liquid felt thick and was so buoyant that Tom and Kate could just about float. We remained there until our skin was red and wrinkled. Cally even insisted on bringing her soap and shampoo and having a good scrub. One of the more recent pictures I had seen of this area had showed my old friend Mo Anthoine smiling from a steamy pool. He was a talented climber who was tragically to die from a completely unrelated brain tumour. I knew he would have applauded to see I had brought my children here. He had ignored the armchair critics too and lived his short life to the full.

CHAPTER EIGHT

A WALK ON THE WILD SIDE?

'Great things are done when Men & Mountains meet.'

WILLIAM BLAKE

Today was the day we were to strike out on foot into the Baltoro region and the loads for the porters were being prepared. Ibrahim, watched by over 120 pairs of eager eyes, hoisted the spring balance to shoulder level as a neatly packaged load was attached to the rusting hook dangling beneath. I could see the big man's biceps tighten as he took the weight with one arm. Ashraf peered at the scale and gave a nod of assent as the baggage was unhitched and carefully laid in a row alongside the others.

Word had gone out as soon as our party reached Skardu, nearly a week ago, that a late-season expedition would be looking for porters at Tongol. Many of the faces greeting us out of the darkness on the night we arrived were men from the surrounding villages who had come down the valley hoping they would be hired. One porter told me he had walked all the way from Skardu on the off-chance that there might be few days work for him. Now there were over 120 men, grouped in little huddles, some sitting cross-legged on the dusty ground, others standing smoking, all waiting to see if there was a job for them.

Portering is a lucrative form of employment by the standards of this area where often the only other option is to scrape a living out of the fields. The job is strictly government-controlled so all treks have to pay a standard rate, which not only covers their wage but stipulates the food porters are to receive along the route – rations include tea, atta flour for chapattis, some meat and cigarettes. The distance they can carry a load in a day is also set out but, most importantly, they are not allowed to carry over 25 kilograms (55 pounds), hence the careful measurement of the loads.

The babble of voices from Ashraf's personal crew as they moved into action at first light had woken me from my warm bed. I lay there reluctant to rise from my cosy cocoon but sensing the buzz of activity outside. All I could see was a little square of blue-grey sky through one of the tent's ventilator panels, as I had zipped the big doorway closed when a storm blew up in the night. I felt for my glasses in the side pocket of the inner tent and found the damp had left my lenses misty with condensation. After giving them a quick polish with the corner of my T-shirt I was soon seeing the world blur-free and in focus again. Beside me, Kate, who had managed to do a somersault in the night, was completely upside down in her sleeping bag. Tom was lying slightly across his mat and dozing gently. I could see his chest rise and fall beneath my duvet jacket, which he had sneaked on before going to bed.

Our clothes for the day were laid neatly to one side so I reached forward deftly and pulled on my fleece top. The bulge in madam's sleeping bag made a noise and a hot, flushed face appeared and declared instantly, 'Daaad, I want a new name. I don't want to be Kate any more'. I feigned deafness to give me time to put on my long socks and fleece trousers before being forced to reply to this clearly very pressing matter. 'Whhhy?' I echoed, already knowing what the answer would be.

'Because I do.' Her standard reply came with resentful force. There had to be some logic in that. I ran through every girl's name I could think of. In the end she could not decide between Caitlin and Sarah so, thankfully, opted to remain Kate for the time being.

I unzipped the tent to find the field covered in white powder as though a huge flour sieve had been emptied over us. The dust had been brought in by the night storm and lay like a thin layer of snow, except where the porters' shoes had scuffed up the dry black earth once more.

I stepped out into a slightly overcast morning and noticed the Hushe boys were hovering. As each of our team got up for breakfast they would swing into action, dismantle the tents and pack them into loads.

As the canvas came down I dressed Tom and Kate for our day's trek in walking boots, thick socks, shorts, T-shirts and a fleece to cover it all up, at least until the sun came out. The breakfast gong sounded at a timely moment. I had just discovered that either Tom, Kate or both had managed to fill our tote bags with sand and grit, which meant I would have to empty them out and start packing all over again. The lure of breakfast kept my short temper in check. We sat down to tea, chapattis, jam and eggs. 'Miluk, Sah?' It was Abdul with his jug for the tea. 'I want miluk, miluk,' cried Tom and Kate in unison. I surveyed the activity around me. The BBC crew looked and acted like real trekkers for the first time as they rushed around packing totes, stuffing sleeping bags and rolling up mats. I could tell they were excited to be on the move again, although they tried to play it cool as they sauntered in for breakfast. 'Hi beautiful, ready to go?' Chris Terrill asked Kate, squeezing himself into a space next to her. Kate, who had already asked all of them to marry her, grinned at the attention.

David and Cath had been making their way over for breakfast when they were waylaid by a stream of local people seeking treatment for a variety of ailments. Parents and friends of the sick, who had been hovering nervously at the edge of camp, finally brought their children forward, realizing this was the last chance they had before we left. An impromptu surgery was under way in the corner of the field, a state of affairs that was to occur in every settlement we passed through. As soon as word went out that Western doctors were travelling in the party, the sick made a beeline for them. While David and Cath were reluctant to use up too many of our medical supplies on the way in, just in case they were needed later, they did not want to turn people away if they could make a difference. For them, the depressing thing was the number of cases they could do little about because they needed either hospital treatment or a long cycle of specialist drugs. Most worrying of all were the tuberculosis cases, which they did not have the facilities to treat but knew with horrid certainty would spread when the sufferers returned to their villages.

David and Cath's dedication to medicine had impressed me when we all travelled to Everest in 1994. However, there was one occasion when even David's gentlemanly and soothing bedside manner was stretched to the limit. Tom, Kate and I were at base camp and we had woken one morning to find the mess tent in chaos, a table and chair broken and blood everywhere. A night spent indulging in coarse, locally distilled whisky had resulted in a drunken brawl among the top Sherpas over money. The worst of the fighting had been between the sirdar and one of the specialist high-altitude Sherpas. David and I had hunted down the two men, concerned not only for their wellbeing but also to prevent the fight from starting up all over again. The Sherpa, Dorje, had broken a knuckle and cracked a number of bones in his hand. As David prepared to get down to work I sat Tom and Kate next to the pain-racked man, knowing this would put him at his ease. Dorje hung his head sheepishly as David filled him full of painkillers and set the broken bones, arranging his sling in a way that would make punching virtually impossible.

We discovered his victim, Kilu, cowering among the packed ice on the floor of the kitchen tent. He had been accused of pocketing money supposed to have been spent on the Sherpas' food and his bruised and blackened lips, swollen to triple their normal size, suggested he had come off worse. David led this sorry figure through to his makeshift mess-tent surgery to get a closer look. Gently examining his patient he found both lips were pitted with jagged bits of broken teeth. He cleaned him up carefully, pulling the remnants out of the tender flesh as kindly as possible, and was just completing the task when the sirdar, with tearful eyes, produced a selection of knocked-out teeth wrapped up in a filthy rag. After the fight he had apparently crept back and picked them up off the floor. In almost apologetic tones David explained that, once broken off, even the most advanced Western dental procedures could not put them back.

On that occasion Cath took a back seat to her husband but there was no-one I would rather have to care for the children than her. I would jokingly wind her up sometimes by calling her 'nurse', which always whipped up her fiery Welsh blood. This came about after she told me one night as we sat in the mess tent about how mothers would bring their children into her surgery and, after she had examined and prescribed for their ailments, tell their offspring to, 'Say thank you to the nurse'. I think that is what you would call women being their own worst enemy. In her diary, written at K2 base camp, Alison noted that it was also a woman who asked her how it felt to be the only woman in maybe thirty men: 'I said I was so used to being one of many [men] I hadn't really even noticed'.

Since her death I have received hundreds of letters from people all over the world and there has not been one that has actually criticized her for what she did. The majority of them have drawn inspiration in their own lives from the fact that she continued to climb at the highest levels and have two children as well. On the couple of television shows I did before we left, the comments coming from some members of the audience were absolutely frightening. One man actually spoke of 'allowing' his wife to do something, as if she was some sort of chattel. You could see the rest of the audience bristling at that. Despite the fact that it is 1995, not 1795, people have in the past said to me, 'Why do you allow her to do it?' My response has always been the same: that nobody owns anybody and women should have the same opportunities as men.

Cath and David eventually escaped to join us for breakfast and no sooner had we swallowed our last mouthful and drained our mugs than the table, chairs and kitchen utensils were whipped away and turned, like everything else, into 25-kilogram loads. Only when all the weighing was finished did Ashraf start the job of choosing the eighty men he wanted. Unlike his personal team of strapping boys from the Hushe valley most of the porters from the local area were small, dark and wiry with the distinctive flat-faced, wide-eyed Tibetan look. They treated the Hushe boys with nervous deference. I liked the wild arrogance of the elite Hushes – they gave us absolute loyalty as their employers but, I was sure, could be fiercely cut-throat if necessary. As well as being his senior cook team, Ashraf used these distinctive tall tribesmen for the plum jobs of carrying the BBC equipment and David and Cath's medical kit. They were a tightknit bunch but Kate's minder Ibrahim was clearly the ringleader.

As the main expedition organizer in the Karakoram region Ashraf had employed many of the local men before. His concern was to make sure that he chose an even mix from all the villages in the Shigar valley. If he didn't, he could fuel bad feeling that might lead to lingering resentment and blood feuds. Each of the five or six main village groups remained in their own tight little circle, waiting to be selected. Ashraf would nod his head or point at the ones he wanted and their names would be written down in an expedition account-book by Abdul.

Instead of the conical woven baskets and headstraps worn by Nepali porters, the Baltis used old-fashioned but effective pack frames with shoulder straps. A few had once been commercially made from alloy tubing and nylon tape but the vast majority were locally manufactured from bits of rope, wood and the odd rusty nail. They looked pretty uncomfortable but the suspicious way each one guarded his own model suggested they were considered prized possessions. The porters moved forward and picked their up their loads, which were written into Ashraf's book next to their names. Each man stuffed his sleeping blankets between the load and his back to act as padding and strapped his own gear on top. All wore the traditional two-piece shalwar qamis, with only the lucky ones owning a pair of plastic trainers. The rest had either cheap sandals or the ubiquitous oversized cut-down Wellington boots. Those porters carrying consumables such as bags of rice, flour or paraffin would be paid off along the route as the supplies were used up. All we had to carry was a small rucksack – called a day sack – containing our drinks, waterproofs and cameras.

Ashraf gave a signal and the chaotic throng unwound and set off in single file along the narrow path before us. Tom, Kate and I and the rest of the team were about to follow them when the local policeman, who had been watching the proceedings, announced he would like to entertain us to yet another tea ceremony to send us off in style. Our day sacks were dropped reluctantly and we all trudged after him to the police post. It was an understatement to say we were impatient to be on the move, particularly as we saw our porters disappearing, but realizing the honour accorded by such a farewell we made the most of the tea and biscuits offered. A round of handshakes eventually saw us on our way.

Tom, sporting a navy-blue turban and carrying Brown Bear under his arm, struck out on his own. He was perfectly at home kicking up the dust in front of us, imagining he was his favourite cartoon character, Tintin. In the same spirit, I decided it would be interesting to follow in the footsteps of early explorers such as Sir Martin Conway, who organized the first major expedition to the Baltoro in 1892, or the Italian Duke of Abruzzi, who attempted K2 in 1909 but turned back on what later became known as the Abruzzi ridge.

At this point in her journey, Alison would still have been on a jeep and would have only started on foot when she scrambled up the cliffs to Askoli. As she began her walk from Askoli she described how impressed she was with the country:

Saturday 17 June. This time last week I was on the Underground from Heathrow to Euston – tired as ever. Now I'm still tired as ever but in hot, dry and dusty Pakistan. I have been surprised and amazed by how nice some bits can be. To me it isn't as fantastic as Tibet, where I loved the contrast between flat plateau and mountain. Here I know the scenery will get more and more impressive in its jagged harshness...Today it's hot. Woke about 4.20 a.m. and fell back to sleep until tea arrived at 4.55 a.m. Packed my day sack and my barrel, then breakfast. The porters – hard-working as ever – took down the tent. By 6.30 a.m. we were on our way. Many stops for water, blister-easing and rest until, finally, lunch at 1.00 p.m. – crackers, tuna and tinned fruit. Half an hour's rest in the shade then on again.

The land was dotted with golden cone-shaped stooks and bundles of wheat, laid out in overlapping concentric circles. Now the crop had been harvested you could see the irrigation channels that criss-crossed each field, which were controlled by simple stone sluicegates. We moved on up the steep, stony track – it could have been any European country path on a warm autumnal day with the leaves on the small outcrops of trees glowing brown, orange and yellow in the sun. That was, until you lifted your eyes to the jagged ice-topped mountains all around – nowhere else has quite the savagery of the Karakoram panorama. We strolled on, trying to ignore our film crew who, at this stage, seemed to be under our feet continually. The next village was Surungo, a little larger and with a few more buildings than Tongol, some of which had quite complicated summer dwellings constructed on the flat roofs of the houses. At the far end of the village was a high wall finished with a spiky lattice of dried thorns. It reminded me of the original Zulu kraals in South Africa and was obviously used to protect a highly prized crop. I peered inside. It was full of carrots!

The fields of Askoli lay below us. Even from here the village looked scruffy, run-down and untidy. I had not taken to this place and wanted to get through it as fast as possible. A young porter walking close by turned out to be a local boy and pointed out the main water supply as we descended towards dwellings. I was not really listening and let his fractured English flow over my head, cocking an ear to Tom instead, who was holding my hand and chatting away about the views below. 'The people look just like ants,' he chirped, looking down at the wheat being cut. 'It is so hard to believe that those are real people – they look just like models.'

It was only when I heard the sound of crashing water that my curiosity about what the young porter was saying was aroused. We rounded the next hillock to find a rushing stream tumbling down a rocky crevice on to smooth polished stones. A man-made channel diverted most of the water away from its natural path into a spraying spout that fell about 3 feet to a flat washing area. This, he said, was the local laundry. Judging from what I had seen on our previous afternoon's visit it was little used.

We continued to follow the path cut by the stream and saw that it was also being used to power a small mill. The water from a deep pool ran along a slot gouged out of a log like a telegraph pole, which was wedged almost vertically so the water fell with maximum force. Our porter kindly fed our interest by pushing open a tiny door in the low round stone building and allowing us to have a look inside. The water drove a wooden paddle in a channel on the floor and this, in turn, rotated stone discs that ground the wheat into fine flour — a method mankind has been using since he learnt to harvest nature's bounty.

I marched on smartly with Tom, David, Cally and Suds. We remembered the hassle Tom had received during our last visit and did not want to have to run the gauntlet of the village children again. We thought we had escaped the worst this time and could just see the village beginning to drop away into empty countryside when Ibrahim came bounding up with Kate. 'Excuse me, Sah, Mr James, but the mayor would like to offer you tea.' Another tea ceremony. Great.

Once more we found ourselves ushered around a grubby corner into the mayor's suite of rooms. This time, at least, we escaped the worst of the choking smoke by supping our tea on the balcony. As guest of honour I was slotted into the back corner and once again found myself balancing on the garden chair. The tea this time had huge leaves that were left to stew in the pot as the china tea cups were brought out once more. Two cups seemed mandatory to be polite, so we quickly downed the hot brew. Everyone then looked at me expectantly so I rose majestically and made my excuses. Unfortunately our idea of a quick getaway was blown when nature called for cameraman Chris Openshaw. 'Is there a toilet handy?' he asked quickly. The request stunned us all with its optimism. The mayor looked bemused, hands were pointed and Chris was gone. We sat back down, more tea was poured and the mayor's dulcet tones began again. Eventually a pale and exhausted-looking Chris returned. Professional as ever, he picked up his camera and shot the final reels before following us outside.

We put our heads down and stomped out of the village,

determined there would be no more hold-ups. The local children, who had a horrible habit of standing close up to our faces, came running after us rubbing their thumbs and forefingers together, whining, 'Money? Pens?' Others opened their mouths and pointed down their throats. They had learned how to tug at the heart- and purse-strings of trekkers over the years with callous efficiency. Suds and I minded Tom but the leering faces continued and I could see him frowning with anger and frustration. I called over Ibrahim and asked him to do something to get them to stop. A few choice words in the local language from this towering father of six seemed to do the trick.

We passed the dilapidated village boundary wall and the natural rock closed in around us. Mottled and brown, it drove us into a gully and blocked out the light as we picked our way across scattered stones. The climber in me could not help thinking it would be a good place to 'boulder' for a few days. All you would need would be shorts, rock boots, a brush to clear the lichen and dirt and a chalk bag to keep your hands dry – no ropes or equipment would be necessary because you could safely jump off everything. Bouldering was something Alison and I both used to enjoy very much and we found it a good way to train. I wondered if she, too, had noticed this spot's potential.

I thought back to when she had first moved in with me at the age of eighteen. I had a large black-and-white Border collie called Rupert that I had rescued from the local dog pound. Alison adored him and he doted on her. Every morning as I drove to work in Matlock Bath I would drop them off on the gritstone moor of Black Rock in Derbyshire's Peak District to climb, run and scramble. Alison and Rupert would spend all day out there, no matter what the weather. She would appear home as it started to get dark flushed with excitement and health, Rupert close behind her. I am sure that dog thought I had got her just for him.

That's what made Alison the great climber she was – that absolute feeling of being at home among the mountains. She changed, chameleon-like, when she went into the wilderness. She wasn't happy in towns and cities; she could cope quite well, but she was never the same person. You could see her totally relax when she got out of a cable car or when she left civilization, even in Britain. The Germans of the 1930s would have called her a 'child of nature'. That was Alison. She became part of where she was, assimilating into the mountain environment rather than standing out as most people do.

That instinct came out of the womb with her, as did the drive that took her to the top. She never had to prove anything, she knew how good she was and always knew what she could do. The only time you would see it was when people tried to suggest she could not climb. If she was on a crag, she would simply demonstrate it – nothing overt, she just climbed and showed her style. I remember a time when we were climbing in France and encountered a loud American girl done up in all the latest clinging Lycra clothing, who was what we in Yorkshire would call 'all mouth and no trousers'. Alison said nothing as this girl broadcasted her skills and climbing experience, totally unaware of who she was talking at. However, as soon as Alison started to climb I saw how much it had riled her. Every move she made was a perfect example of the style, grace and elegance of the climber. This simple demonstration cut through the American's bombast and taught her a valuable lesson: never judge a book by its cover...

The valley opened out and we walked across a sandy floor, overshadowed on either side by huge cliffs that seemed to slice for an eternity into the grey sky. Their buttresses criss-crossed the path ahead; it looked unlikely walking terrain but the porters simply pressed on so we followed suit, the soft sand underfoot making it heavy going. We passed distinctive humbug-striped rock as the line of porters began to snake along a narrow cliff path that rose some 45 metres (almost 150 feet) above the valley floor. We wound our way steeply upwards around the mountainside until the path began a precarious descent down a scree slope. The porters sidestepped downwards and we copied them, conscious that loose stones could fall away from the hillside in a mini avalanche of rubble. As ever when the going got rough, Suds and I kept Tom between us, while Kate was safely tucked up on Ibrahim's broad back. Ibrahim, who had made this journey countless times before, was simply smiling at Kate's usual banter. On this occasion it appeared to revolve around her toy dog Kipper, as I could see his soft foam-filled shape being waved about under Ibrahim's nose.

The path became rocky again but still hugged the riverside. Across the valley lay the last of the summer-only settlements, Ste Ste, where we could see people in the field just beginning to harvest. Ashraf had told the porters to stop at the first stream for lunch but, when we approached, there was no-one in situ. He was not pleased and accelerated as only a fit and angry Hunza can to see what had gone wrong. We were supposed to continue along a series of slippery stepping stones by the river but, like so much else, these had been washed away by the recent storms. Instead, army contractors had carved a stone staircase up one side of the rocks and down the other. Obvious care was needed and in single file we clambered up and along the stone ledges.

As we crested the bulge of loose rocks we heard voices and saw below us eighty bemused-looking porters and our cook team. Ashraf was in the centre looking a little more relaxed. 'I am so sorry Mr James, that the porters did not stop earlier.' He was flushed with embarrassment. He explained that the porters, finding the first stream had dried up, had continued on to the second to get a clean water supply. Even though we were now only half-an-hour from our overnight camp we were happy to drop our day sacks and camera bags and consume mugs of tea and biscuits. The cooks had two mini portions of scrambled eggs ready for Tom and Kate as they had gained some fresh eggs in Askoli. The children wolfed these down as only hungry explorers can. We continued our descent and rounded the corner to see a huge flat area of sand and scrubby vegetation stretching into the distance. Cliffs loomed over to one side while the river bounded the other. This was to be our camp for the night. The porters dropped their loads and scuttled off to gather dry wood, sticks and even leaves for fires. Our tents went up and mattresses and sleeping bags were soon laid out. I put the children into warm clothes as the temperature began to drop and left them to play around the mess tent while I went off to take some photographs. I discovered later from Alison's diary that she had even managed a dip on her trek:

Saturday 17 June. We stopped by two fantastic blue pools. I stripped to my bathing costume (this always comes in handy and I have carried it in my sack ever since going climbing on Sundays in the Peak District). I dipped and swam three times — grand. Then on to a river-basket crossing and camp. There is a mutiny because there is no good water. Eventually one of the porters had to walk for two hours for it. I rest in my tent at 6.15 p.m. and am woken at 8.15 p.m. for dinner. Now it's 9.30 p.m. I've not felt strong today — hot, upset stomach and sore feet.

There was a definite hierarchy to the porter huddles. Low stone walls were used to keep the wind at bay and the better camps had elaborate fireplaces crafted from simple stones. The best site went to Ibrahim and his Hushe boys and so on down to the poorest-looking Askoli team, who ended up with very sparse cover indeed. Old cans or saucepans, depending on the status and wealth of the team, sat on the fires. My Hushe favourites were brewing the Balti staple of salt tea which, to someone used to the stuff that comes from supermarket-bought teabags, looked appalling. I watched them take the long, black, ribbon-like leaf from a roll of brown paper and add the strands to boiling water. The concoction was agitated with a wooden stick rubbed aggressively between two palms until the solution became a deep blood-red. Into this were added salt, butter and a little dried milk powder. The result, with its disconcerting buttery, leafy aroma, was held out for me to try. I politely but firmly declined. To go with this they had small cakes of flat round bread, known locally as 'Khurba'. Ibrahim broke off a large piece and handed to me. It tasted remarkably like American sourdough bread and I gobbled it down, only then realizing how hungry I was.

I returned to the mess tent for my own evening meal — more pasta, tomato and tuna for the vegetarians and chicken again for the meat-eaters (from a supply of live poultry carried by the porters). By the time we reached the hot drinks, Kate, on Cath's lap, could barely keep her eyes open, while Tom's head was drooping into his mug of tea. It was a cold night but the sky was clear and star-studded, boding well for the morning. I filled their drinks bottles with boiled water and orange powder and stuffed these up their jumpers to take to bed as hot-water bottles. In the morning, when the contents had cooled, they would be drunk.

I fell asleep listening to the crackle and hiss of the porters' fires and the low murmur from the figures around them. Only in bad weather were expedition organizers expected to provide these hardened mountain men with tarpaulins. These were usually flung over a stone wall and held up with a stick, but on clear nights like this they would simply curl up inside their blankets, pile on top of each other like puppies in a basket and go to sleep.

CHAPTER NINE

A NIGHT TO REMEMBER

'There cannot be a crisis next week. My schedule is already full.'
HENRY KISSINGER

'Daaad, Daaad, can I have a tutu?' It was Kate. The first signs of early morning were beginning to seep through the tent door, which I always left open for fresh air. Kate was already wide awake and determined that the rest of us should be as well. 'What's a two-two?' I asked sleepily.

'You know, what you wear for ballet,' she said, jumping on me. I wondered what on earth had prompted thoughts of ballet at 5.30 a.m. in the Baltoro. A few blissful moments of silence followed, then, 'What colour are they?' Her high-pitched voice broke into my slumbers again. It was time to get up.

We dressed and headed out into the dawn glow to the large mess tent for a cup of tea. Gradually, the others joined us around the metal trestle table that had been unfolded for breakfast. Kate, still with ballet on her mind, persuaded Cath to give her a lesson and a flat sandy patch in front of the mess tent was turned into a temporary stage. She pointed and pirouetted to her heart's delight, knowing she had a captive audience.

Breakfast finished, our bags were packed, the porters loaded and we were ready to push on. The clear skies the night before had not lived up to expectations and it was overcast and not very warm. The morning would be spent gaining height. So far, the scare stories that had been bandied about before we left Britain – that the rivers would be impassable, the temperatures would be too cold and the altitude too high to be safe for the children – had failed to be realized. David and Cath had found it virtually impossible to get unbiased opinions from the mountaineering establishment about the risks involved and, when they were aired, it was usually in the media rather than to them, the people who would most have benefited from expert help. The simple fact seemed to be that the fag end of autumn, when we were travelling, was when the weather in the region was at its most stable – even the nights were not as cold as they could be. We were experiencing temperatures from 23 °F down to 14 °F (-5 to -10 °C) but that was nothing to the -4 to -22 °F (-20 to -30 °C) on our Everest trip. At this time of year the rivers, which often form one of the biggest dangers on the journey, are at their lowest and the crossings reasonably safe. Even Alison, travelling just a few months before us at the end of the Pakistani spring, had a much more demoralizing time than we did.

Monday 19 June. It was raining hard and had been for a while. I got everything off the floor as the groundsheet was leaking and I didn't want things getting wet. I remembered back to the summer of 1993, camping in the Alps with night after night of wet floors and wet kit…It never really brightened today – just kept raining – when the sun did break through it was only on the other side of the valley. My washing is wet. I am missing Tom and Kate desperately.

Tuesday 20 June. Woke about 5.00 a.m. and realized we were supposed to be getting up at 4.30 a.m. It was raining hard and not a lot was happening. I packed my barrel and my sack on the assumption we'd move anyway – however most folks seemed to have other ideas. Breakfast – cornflakes and bread. The cereal was almost palatable if the hot milk was put in a bowl and left to cool first. Cups of hot orange and Ovaltine. I can't stand the coffee here…It rained and rained more and harder. Finally at 8.45 a.m. the decision was to go. Within five minutes the sun was out and I was down to shorts and T-shirt. Before we'd been in Gortex, fleece, hats and gloves.

Next, a large river crossing – I tried to go high and avoid taking my boots off (I'd seen the porters in front walking lower down) but the flow was

too much. I descended and ended up to my knees in freezing water with
brown, cold sludge gushing past me and my boots tied firmly around my
neck. Onto the sand, one more stream to cross, then back on with my boots.
On to camp, tea and bed by 9.30 p.m. I have a blister on my heel.

Until a decade or so ago this route to K2 through Concordia – the
junction of the Godwin Austen glacier and the upper Baltoro glacier
and traditionally the last camping ground before K2 base camp – was
considered to be one of the hardest treks in the world. But the conflict
between Pakistan and India for control of the Siachen area has changed
all that. The Pakistani army, involved in frontier disputes, has installed
small outposts dotted along the Baltoro and set up a major base at
Paiju. Now, instead of using scores of porters to move their loads,
the army has started to use cheaper and more sturdy Zanskar ponies.
Having four legs instead of two they require wider paths and have
forced the military to improve the tracks, so the whole trek is now a
great deal more reasonable for everybody.

We strolled along a flat sandy track, taking it at a steady pace as we
were by now walking at over 3050 metres (10 000 feet) and altitude
problems were a possibility. The rock was streaked with wild natural
patterns that took my mind off the rigours of the Biafo glacier to come.
We would soon be replacing the solid rock underfoot with shifting dirt
and unpredictable ice patches. Just like all glaciers, this one had receded
well beyond anything the early explorers would recognize, leaving a
wasteland of rocky sludgy debris that looked rather like redundant mine
slag heaps. What ice that could be seen was well disguised under heaps
of stones. The overwhelming image was of a drab landscape cast in every
possible shade of grey. The approach was steep, so it was probably the
outside curve of the glacier where it met its final end. The surface was
loose but the little path picked the safest route possible between one
solid bed of stones and the next. The team spread out as each of us
concentrated on following it through this potential accident blackspot.

From further ahead a party of European and American trekkers
came plunging towards us. Their English leader was sweating

profusely and pointing with dismay after his disappearing line of porters. He tried to pull himself together and managed a weak smile as we drew level. 'You have a long walk in front of you,' he shouted. I thought it was a pretty inane comment and riposted, 'Now that is a surprise'. My wit was lost on him as he rushed on, shouting and gesticulating wildly for his porters to halt. Not much chance of that, I thought, aware that when a trek turns and heads for home the porters often fly off to get back as quickly as possible. We had passed their grinning porters earlier, on the far bank of the Biafo, and they had been moving pretty swiftly even then. I guessed they had no intention of stopping until they reached the 'flesh pots' of Askoli.

Behind the panicking leader was a second lad and a tousle-haired girl, neither of whom looked very happy. I said 'Hello' and was just about to strike up a conversation when I was distracted by a crashing sound behind and below me. It was their other chum, now trying to cut a new path. I have never understood why anyone, no matter how experienced or strong they think they are, should want to try to rush across this type of unstable terrain. One wrong step and you could go crashing through soft ice or slip and break an ankle. Perhaps coming across a six-year-old boy looking relaxed and completely at home on the glacier had had an unsettling effect. Great physical strength and fitness count for little out here. Success is in the mind – and rule one is not to be intimidated or overawed by the size and savagery of the mountain environment all around you.

I caught up with the rest of my mob over the main rise as Ashraf was dispatching his cook team off in front to set up the stoves for lunch at the convenient oasis called Korophon at 3109 metres (10 200 feet) – although this was the name given to a boulder that sticks out like sore thumb another three-quarters of a mile further on. We were to eat near a small army base and observation post. The stones underfoot became larger and the once-icy folds flatter. Much sooner than expected we passed onto flat sand dotted with shrubs and trees that indicated that we were approaching a spring. The army posts in this area were supposed to be 'invisible' but this one was clearly evident, squatting as it did in a small dip and surrounded by potted plants. If that was not a big enough giveaway, the field toilet had a more pungent smell than any ancient midden.

Lunch was already waiting for us: biscuits, chapattis, cheese, tinned sardines, fruit, tuna and jam, with hot milky tea to wash it all down. After our morning walk it tasted delicious. We relaxed and were lucky enough to be able to enjoy the indulgence of watching the porters pack up after us while Tom played with the BBC soundman Adrian Bell in a nearby stream. The weather remained overcast as we set off again, eagerly awaiting the box-car ride ahead that would take us over one of the flowing torrents. We followed the boulder-strewn banks of the river Braldu until we came to a huge sand and pebble beach at the point where it converged with the Dumordo river. This used to be one of the biggest hurdles to gaining access to the area. You had to scramble along the bank of the Dumordo for a couple of miles to reach a flimsy wooden bridge where the river became narrower. In high water this would often be washed away and even longer detours were required. More recently, a cable bridge (known as the Flying Fox) was installed by the military. Local Askoli henchmen charge trekkers a fee to cross, although its actual maintenance is left to...'Inshallah' – God's will.

One of the advance porters pointed us up river as most of the Baltis whipped off their plastic trainers, slung them around their necks and waded through the swollen water to the far bank. We continued to plod along the shifting sand until hawk-eyed David Collier let out a cry. He had spotted the cable in the distance. Two wires had been slung across the water. One was for use during the springtime floods and there was another, lower down, that we were going to cross on. We all clambered onto the stone platform where the thick hawser cable was fixed firmly into huge iron-eyed pins sunk into the bedrock. Slung underneath the cable on a single pulley was a simple three-sided wooden box, the size of a large armchair. It was made out of rough wood on planks about 6 inches wide and an inch thick, and was attached to the pulley by four lengths of stiff wire rope. The main cable sloped down to the far bank 60 to 70 feet away, where a huge stone monolith secured the other end. A thin tattered rope was attached to each end to help speed the box across and bring it back from the other side.

The open end of the box faced the opposite bank. Several grinning Balti porters grabbed it firmly and with gentle care lifted Tom into the back. I perched as nonchalantly as possible, feet dangling from the open end. The Balti grins widened, their big white teeth flashing, as they let go and we hurtled towards the foam. The main cable took up the strain as we accelerated downwards, then up again. 'Yahooo...' shouted Tom and I echoed him. I still do not know who felt the biggest kid. What a brilliant adrenaline rush – the Balti answer to a theme park 'white knuckle' ride!

Ibrahim, impassive as ever, brought Kate across. He kept her on his back and sat stiffly as he made the short journey while she thrashed about in her carrier in excitement. All 18 stones of David Collier then stepped on board, amusing the assembled porters as the cable stretched and dipped ever closer to the tumbling water. Unfazed, he went across, camera clicking. Then it was the turn of Cath and Cally, who rode across together. The Baltis smirked mischievously – they thought this was when the screams of terror and panic would start. However, they were sorely disappointed to discover that the two women were made of good adventurous stock and took it all in their stride with glee.

The slog down the other bank of the Dumordo river was a touch bland by comparison and we reached Bardumal (3368 metres/11 044 feet), where we were to camp, just as the weather started to turn misty and damp. The sandy shelf was narrow and the rock walls above overhung it steeply. The wind started to pick up and down came the rain. Ashraf issued the poorest porters with tarpaulins made from old fly sheets. It did not look as though they had a very good night in front of them.

The children did not fancy our evening meal of dahl and rice so Little Ibrahim, the cook, made them special bowls of scrambled eggs. Kate just picked at hers but Tom scoffed the lot and then polished off

Kate's, while she tucked into a couple of muesli bars. It was such a cool and wet night that as soon as everyone had finished eating we drifted off to our tents early.

'Dad.' I felt a tug at my T-shirt. It was Tom. 'I don't feel well, Dad – I think I'm going to be sick.' I awoke to pitch blackness but fumbled on my glasses out of habit and shook the deep sleep from my eyes. I was used to getting up in the night for the children at home, but this was different. I switched on my head torch in time to see Tom vomit violently into his cupped hands. It seemed to happen in ghostly slow motion in the pale light. I passed him over our large damp flannel and was reaching for the clean matching towel when he was sick again, this time in a most impressive way. It was hard to believe a bowl and a half of scrambled eggs and half a litre of fresh orange juice could amount to so much. Tom had been sleeping on the far side of the tent, so he managed to be sick all over my down jacket which he was using as a pillow, as well as over all the spare fleeces for him and Kate and most of the small waterproof bags containing Kate's spare day clothes.

When he finally stopped I wiped him down and stood him in the far corner of the tent, away from all the chaos. He shivered with the cold so I pulled one of my spare fleece tops over his T-shirt and then tried to continue my general cleaning up. By this time the flannel and towel were disgusting and I was starting to feel none too well myself, so I decided they could wait to be washed out until the morning. I threw them out of the tent and down by the river. Thankfully, Kate was still asleep, completely oblivious to the commotion. I rearranged all the sleeping bags into a big double bed by zipping the bottom halves together. Then I used Tom's still wet but not too smelly sleeping bag as a quilt. He had obviously recovered and was feeling much better when, as I was about to slot him in, he announced proudly, 'I have been sick on everything. The only thing that I have missed was your spare clothes and anyway I am going to sleep in your sleeping bag.' His cockiness was too much. My temper erupted in a tired outburst and I called him every name under the sun, plus a few I am sure he did not understand. His body stiffened and his little face looked up at mine in disbelief. He went deathly pale and his lips quivered. I felt terrible. I picked him up and hugged him and put him into my sleeping bag. A muffled sound came from underneath the covers. 'Sorry,' he whispered, gulping back the tears.

'It's not your fault. The eggs were probably bad,' I answered, also in a whisper, feeling terribly guilty. Was it just an upset stomach or the first telltale sign of altitude problems? It was time to get a second opinion and to wake up Cath, who was fast asleep in the next-door tent. I stuck my boots on unlaced and hopped across to grab what I hoped was her foot. It was, and within what seemed like seconds she joined me in the family tent. Immediately alert, she took Tom's pulse, felt his head and took his temperature and, by the time David joined us, had decided it was an upset stomach caused by something he had eaten during the day. Despite her calm reassurances and the sight of Tom's perky face, I was still concerned. We decided to see what tomorrow would bring.

As I slotted myself in between the children I started to worry. Was this the end of the road? If Tom was not well the next day it would have to be back down the valley to the head of the jeep road at Tongol. If he was really poorly in the morning it would be time to break out our emergency satellite phone and call a helicopter to whip him, Kate, Cath and me back to Skardu hospital. I couldn't sleep and lay there, listening to his breathing. The love I had for Tom and Kate shot through me like a bullet. I could not let anything happen to them. I experienced my first and only doubts about the trip. Had I, after all, been pig-headed in insisting that we come?

I thought back to a time at Everest base camp when I had faced a similar dilemma. Alison was on the 'big hill' acclimatizing. By 8.00 p.m. Tom, Kate and I were snuggled down in our sleeping bags. I had read them their favourite bedtime serial from Arthur Ransome's *The Big Six* and it did not take them long to fall asleep. Suddenly I was jolted wide awake by an enormous reverberating thump, which continued to echo in my ears as I sat up. 'Avalanche,' I thought immediately. It sounded enormous and was heading our way from the Khumbu icefall directly behind base camp. A wild, tortured howling, like the noise of a thousand approaching express trains, blasted my ears. Without a second's delay I pulled Kate, who was curled up beside me, sleeping bag and all in between my legs and grabbed Tom, who was on her left, and lifted him in to lie on top of Kate. My left arm locked across both of them. My only thought was that we should all stay together if we were hurled down the mountain or buried under the snow. The thought of them coming round and finding themselves alone with their father dead terrified me more than the possibility of my own imminent death. The ferocious wind blast hit us, the force flattening the tent. The big alloy tent poles bent horizontal and I was pushed down on to the children, my face against the back of Kate's hair as the wind pummelled my back. It seemed strong enough to push us off the mountain and all I could do was grimace and hold on tighter. 'I must keep the children together at all costs,' was the only thought running through my head. Mercifully, the thunder of falling snow did not follow. The blast passed and silence fell. It can only have lasted thirty seconds at most and Tom and Kate were still half asleep. I returned them to their beds and tucked the hot-water bottles back around them.

Venturing outside the intense cold hit me like a punch in the face and caught at the back of my throat. It was lower than -4 °F (-20 °C) and the air was full of tiny glistening ice crystals. The glacier and boulders as far as the eye could see were covered in sparkling diamante white and the camp had an eerie glow. It looked beautiful but I noticed immediately that two of the big research tents had been flattened and bulldozed down the glacier by the blast. Luckily all the sleeping tents had escaped and everyone was alive. The cold was beginning to bite painfully and once everyone was accounted for we all headed back to bed. After that, every noise had me leaping up anxiously, particularly as I heard the roar and crump of several smaller avalanches in the distance. I sat in the dark, looking at my children, who were oblivious to the danger, sleeping peacefully. It had not been their choice to come here; they were too young for that. How would I ever forgive myself if anything happened to them? That night at Everest base camp had seemed endless. With morning came the sun and the clear-up and rebuilding operation. The doubts that had crept out in the dark of night were not forgotten but were put in perspective.

As every parent appreciates, your view on life changes when your first child is born. I found tremendous pleasure when Alison had Tom and loved him intensely like any parent would, although I found it difficult to have a great deal of interest in him when he first came home a little pink bundle from hospital. Alison was then a full-time mother while I was out working and Tom was often asleep when I got home. He was an ideal baby who did not cause much trouble and I remember few restless nights. Both Alison and I wanted another child and when Kate came along we were delighted but it suddenly made me realize I didn't know Tom at all. That was one of the reasons I thoroughly enjoyed the first year I spent a lot of time with the children – 1993 – but, even then, I wasn't left with them all the time: Alison's climbing probably didn't encompass more than a couple of weeks away from the family, spread over the year. We would both give each other space; some days I would take off into the hills and go climbing on my own and that continued right up to the last fortnight I ever saw Alison alive. On the first Sunday she was back after Everest I managed to sneak out of our cabin to spend a couple of hours mountain-biking high up in the Grey Corries.

Alison had continued to climb after Tom was born – just a few months after his birth she climbed the north face of the Droites in the French Alps – but she did not find it so easy with Kate. Alison was a lot bigger the second time around and found she could not be as active as she would have liked, although that did not stop her running and skiing. For a couple of years she gave up regular climbing and devoted herself to the children but gradually things changed as they got older and we both became restless and wanted something different. I wanted more time with the children and she wanted more time to climb. We came up with a two- to three-year plan that began with Alison attempting to solo climb the six north faces in the European Alps and ended with Everest itself.

It meant I took on the role of 'new man', although personally I have never understood the term. I looked after the children while Alison was on the mountains but, whenever possible, we would all travel together and only in the last six months did Alison's climbing demands take her away on her own. That was when people used to ask me if I was a 'house husband', which always seemed a very odd question. I would drop Tom off at school, take Kate to nursery, then spend the morning on the climbing wall in Fort William and the afternoon skiing at Nevis Range with Kate when she was back from playgroup. If that was being a house husband then it seemed to be an ideal lifestyle and one I know most climbers would have envied. I found I even enjoyed the simple things, like making pasta for tea or dropping Kate off at her new nursery school and seeing her excitement at making new friends. Best of all was watching their two young strong personalities develop.

When I wrote or faxed Alison at Everest and K2 it was of these ordinary things that she wanted to hear. The last letter she received from us was sent out on 16 July – a copy was with her diary when her belongings were retrieved – in which I made sure Tom and Kate had scrawled their distinctive signatures on the bottom.

Hi Alison
Tom and Kate are both fine. At the moment they are lost in a *Tintin* adventure (on video).

You will be just as proud as I was to hear that Tom was presented with a book on the last day of term for his hard work at school. Kate was quite emotional at her end-of-term party for her playgroup but seemed to enjoy her visit to her new nursery school...

Nevis Range decided to open their dry ski slope for the summer so when the weather has not been good I have taken the children skiing. They have enjoyed it and Tom has been working hard at his skiing skills.

On the last day of school Tom was sent home at noon so I

picked him up from school and took him and Kate out to the beach at Arisaig. It was an almost perfect afternoon and early evening. The children swam and the water seemed almost lukewarm. Then it was on to mountain-biking. Tom is getting to be a great little pedaller while Kate still sits behind me regally.

We cycled to Glen Roy on another perfect day last week and, after a picnic lunch, the children took their clothes off and spent ages swimming in the river, climbing and sliding on the rocks. They swore blind that the water was warm — it may have been compared to the river at Bondo in Bregaglia but it felt cold to my hastily dipped toe.

Well that is it, breakfast and mountain-biking calls. Good luck with the weather and your attempt on the summit. As ever, all that matters is that you come back safely.

My thoughts returned to Tom, lying beside me swaddled in fleece and goosedown, and my worries kept me awake until dawn. As soon as it was light enough to see I was up, out and pacing. Tom and Kate slept on. Cath had not had a good night either and as soon as she heard my size-ten boots crunching on the sand she was out of her tent like a shot. Kate could be heard stirring in the tent and I knew she would soon wake Tom. Cath climbed in while I hovered quietly at the entrance. Her face popped out again, smiling. She had been absolutely spot-on last night. All Tom had was an upset stomach that had probably been caused by playing in the polluted stream water at Korophon, where he had built a dam with Adrian. It was probably not helped by the rich bowls of eggs he had hastily gobbled up late the night before. However, Cath wanted to give him an extra couple of hours to be absolutely sure.

I told the anxious assembled team before breakfast about Tom's sickness and my outburst of temper. All it drew was a comment from David that perhaps the 'Grand Fromage' was human after all, even if it ran contrary to popular opinion. Time dragged on and Tom soon got restless and wanted to be up and about. I continued to clean out the tent and had six litre-bottles of fresh orange juice made up for the day to make sure Tom was fully hydrated. Cath gave Tom the full medical works and was still as sure as she could be that she had made the correct diagnosis. She gave Tom some antibiotics and a clean bill of health. We decided on a short-day trek to the next camp to make sure he was not overtired, and that applied to a very relieved Cath and me as well.

CHAPTER TEN

PAIJU

'Such awesome power,
Overwhelms the soul,
Numbs the mind.'

RAJA CHANGEZ SULTAN

I was still concerned about Tom, who looked pale, and vowed that if I saw the slightest deterioration in him we would turn back. At least things were looking better on the weather front: the wind had cleared some high clouds and blue sky was in evidence once more. We set off, nudged along by the gentle breeze, Sudsy and I keeping Tom close to us while a conscientious Cath also hung back to keep an eye on her tender young patient. The fresh air seemed to help and any lingering doubts I had that Tom may have been suffering from altitude-related sickness were dispelled as his old energy started to flow back along with his colour.

After a good four hours of gentle walking, the camp site we were heading for came into view. It was hardly used by the major climbing and trekking groups so it still had a plentiful supply of dry, dead wood and good clean spring water and the sand had not been polluted by human waste as it was at some of the more popular stopping spots. The locals call it 'Gambo Chou' which in Balti means 'dry thorns' and it was situated next to a couple of large polished rocks squatting on the edge of a dry river bed. We pitched all our sleeping tents carefully so that their sloping backs faced into the strong prevailing wind and each one protected the one in front. It was still early by the time we settled in and as soon as the mats, sleeping bags and clothes were arranged the children went off to annoy the BBC crew. I fancied a little bit of space and went off to chat to Ibrahim and his cohorts, camera in hand.

The Hushe men were sitting around an impressive fire about 3 feet across and piled 8 or 9 inches high with crackling twigs. On top of this was a flat stone which served as a bread griddle, for today was baking day. The dough was made up from finely ground flour, a simple raising agent and a pinch of salt. These ingredients were mixed together with water on a rock until they formed a dough, which was then pummelled with much gusto until it was well stretched and aired. The resulting lump was then carried away to be made into what we in Yorkshire call breadcakes – large round baps. The locals shaped theirs into a disc 6 inches in diameter and about an inch thick but the Hushe heavies made theirs a good 4 inches bigger and nearly twice as thick. These were placed carefully onto the gently glowing stone and the guy who stoked the fire turned them over continually until they turned golden brown on both sides. Then came the cunning bit. The bread was removed with hardened fingers and placed on its edge in the ashes in front of the roaring fire, propped against the stones encircling the blaze. After a while it was rotated until each side was covered in grey ash with dark-brown burn marks and only then was it pulled out and stacked, cooled and stored in an old, none-too-clean cotton sack. A newly baked loaf was broken for me to taste – it was even better than the one I had eaten the night before and I felt delighted to be asked to share it. On occasions, such as today, a handful of sun-dried tomatoes, fearsome-looking chillies, red and green peppers and onions were moistened and ground into a paste between two coarse, flat stones, which each porter in turn then scraped up with his bread and consumed with gusto. I passed on that one as well as the salt tea – it certainly looked very different from the trendy Balti food I had seen displayed in our local supermarket in Fort William.

Seeing the porters all sitting around the glowing embers I recalled our own family camp fire suppers when we had been living out of Perkins in the Alps in 1993, and one night in particular. We had been camping at Bondo in the Bregaglia, which is a fantastic area of granite peaks straddling the Swiss—Italian border. Alison had gone to collect north face number four, the Piz Badile, and my old friends Sudsy and Ian 'Spike' Sykes were climbing in the same area. I was on my way home from the village with Tom and Kate when the hot and sweaty duo arrived back. 'She's done it, she's OK and she's on her way,' they shouted across the fields to me. We made our way back to the camp site and cranked up the stoves to prepare the biggest pasta dish I have ever seen for her return. Alison arrived exhausted and hungry but regained her energy as we celebrated her success over our meal, washed down with cup after cup of hot tea.

I returned to our mess-tent supper to find Tom and Kate had just about exhausted the BBC boys, although an interesting mini-drama was about to unfold. Chris Terrill had spent time in the afternoon filming and interviewing David Collier as he sat on the river bank. He was particularly pleased with the light and the content of the interview and thought it was 'a wrap'. As we chatted outside the mess tent before dinner Ashraf appeared at my side and said, 'One of my porters from Dassu has found some tins over by the river and has asked me what he should do with them.' The young porter in question was holding out a pile of shiny metal film cans which, I realized, must have been left behind accidentally. 'Tell him to drop them in the river,' I said in mischief, expecting Chris Terrill to intervene. As the lad walked back towards the water I started to laugh and Ashraf, who had cottoned on to my joke, also began to chuckle. The rest of the BBC team joined in but Andy 'Boy' Thompson, who was in charge of all the film, had not grasped what was going on until David, in an expressionless voice, asked him, 'What are those silver cans that porter is about to throw in the river?' Suddenly realizing the film was heading for an early bath, a panic-stricken Andrew set off in hot pursuit and caught him just as he raised his arm to throw. Perhaps I had been slightly childish but it did illustrate how honest and loyal the Baltis were to Ashraf.

After a quick meal we settled into the family tent and lay listening to the rhythmic drumming, stamping and high-pitched singing of the Hushe boys conducting what sounded like their version of Pink Floyd's

'Dark Side of the Moon'. It had a distinctly metallic ring that suggested they had borrowed the cooking utensils again, but the steady beat was strangely comforting and soon lulled us all to sleep. At this point on her trek, Alison was still struggling with appalling weather.

Wednesday 21 June. Last night it rained and rained and rained – consequently, no early start was made. Around 7.00 a.m. I got up, washed in the stream and packed. The scenery is very austere, not at all like Nepal and for me not as inspiring as Tibet. But it is great to view such famous mountains. Bed 9.15 p.m. It is a lot colder tonight and it's clear – have we seen the end of the rain?

Tom was back to normal the next morning and even scoffed a couple of well-fried eggs with his chapattis for breakfast. Cath gave him his last antibiotic pill to finish the course and he seemed to be looking forward to continuing the trek. I walked over to Ashraf and we stood looking at the sky. The wind was obviously blowing hard in the stratosphere and the big cotton-wool clouds were really scuttling about, only very occasionally letting the sun's rays in on us. Ashraf said to me quietly, 'Sir, Mr James, if the weather improves you can sometimes see K2 along this stretch before we reach the main Baltoro glacier.' This was the first time I had been told it was possible to see the mountain before Concordia, further up the valley and still three or four day's walk away. Ashraf said no more and made no promises but now I knew the possibility existed my eyes scoured the cloud-blotted horizon constantly.

The morning packing was quick again, speeded, perhaps, through practice – or was it the thought of what we might see later in the day? Paiju peak was to our left and looked particularly dramatic with its series of slim rocky ridges culminating in a fine high pinnacle. To its left some snowy tops guarded a horrid-looking gully approach and an awful dirty-grey glacier. Scuttling clouds came down again and the mountain tops disappeared but the sound of hidden water gushing from the glacial melt remained impressive.

My boots clumped along with Tom's quieter footsteps shuffling by my side. There was no need to talk; we were each locked in our own thoughts as our eyes followed the path along the riverside. It twisted and turned until we came to a more pronounced upwards slope across scrubby desert terrain that could belong to any hot arid area of the world. I have seen a few in my time and I suppose it was closest to Utah or Arizona, where I had climbed in the Arches National Park and Indian Creek with Alison, Tom and a very young Kate in 1992. It was at Arches that Alison did her first major solo rock climb on the distinctive leaning red sandstone pinnacle of Owl Rock. She always said in interviews that she started climbing on her own because, as a mother with young children, she did not know when she would have free time in advance and it was always hard to find suitable partners at short notice. But it wasn't just that – after Owl Rock I could see she found the stimulation of solo climbing addictive. On that occasion the weather had been snowing on and off and I remember Tom was annoyed because before he could build sand castles he had to clear away the snow. American families who watched him simply shook their heads in amazement at his hardiness. Alison and I had done a few climbs together but every time we drove up or down to our camping ground, the front diagonal crack on Owl Rock winked at her. One day it was too much and she abruptly asked me to stop. Taking nothing more than an abseil rope for her descent, she powered up it. Her grin when she topped out nearly split her face in half. I tried to photograph her and found I only had two exposures left in the camera. I reeled them off, then stood and admired as I watched a climbing genius find her natural vocation. Her talent against nature: that was how she wanted it to be.

People would always ask Alison why she liked climbing and she never really improved on the ultimate answer given by the early-twentieth-century Himalayan climber, George Mallory. He was sent to America to raise money for an expedition to Everest in the 1920s and at one particular function a very persistent Chicago journalist pestered him with this very question until he turned round and replied, 'My dear fellow, because it's there'.

Alison's other answer was equally simple: 'Because I like standing on the top'. In a way it was a spiritual experience as much as a physical one, but spiritual with a small 's'. If you spend any time in wild places and mountains you can quite easily see why men and women have always gone there to find what they're looking for. Alison found her own inner peace as soon as she went anywhere remote.

We rounded a wide bend and came to a large stream and our lunch stop. The kitchen staff, Little Ibrahim and Abdul, were already boiling water and laying out barrels to use as tables. As we sat down to rest our weary legs I noticed the porters seemed particularly quiet and were looking away from us straight along the valley. The view did not seem to warrant such attention for, although we had just turned the major southern spur of the Paiju peak complex, the clouds were still low. As we sat there, the heavy grey blanket started to lift and the Baltoro's treasures began to unfold. Great Trango, with its various rock satellites, was to our hard left and, as we looked right across Biale, Lhungka, Biage, Black Tooth and Lopsang, the entire Savoie range gradually began to emerge. If I was reading my map correctly, that hard triangle of white and grey still partly covered in clouds was K2.

The others were still talking among themselves. 'I think I can see K2,' I said.

'Where?' was the immediate excited response, although Tom and Kate continued sipping on their orange juice-filled water bottles and hunting out more chocolate biscuits. For the adults, food and drink were immediately forgotten as all turned to the map. Ashraf gave me a wry, knowledgable smile. The compass was whirled and cameras' long lenses primed. Was the wind going to play ball? Were we going to get a sneak preview of the mountain we had all come to see, or would it remain an indistinct shape shrouded in cloud? A mug of sweet milky tea and a chapatti containing sardines and tuna were slipped into my hand but my eyes could not leave the spot where I thought K2 was. The vague but impressive triangular outline was still just visible. I took a sip of my tea; it was hot and burnt my tongue leaving its usual metallic taste. Logic told me that so far from Concordia we would have to be incredibly lucky to get a glimpse of the mountain we had travelled 7000 miles to see, but I couldn't help feeling excited. Almost on cue, the clouds started to roll away before our eyes. My sweaty fingers searched for the camera controls as the grey receded and broke up. From nowhere a hole appeared in the dense cloud and spread upwards to reveal K2, around 25 miles away, in all its breathtaking glory.

'Tom, Kate, come and look at this,' I called. They recognized the urgency in my voice and stopped what they were doing. 'What you've got to do, Tom, is to look carefully over there,' I indicated. 'Look to the right first. Now, look about the middle of the mountains we can see.' He followed my finger to the horizon. 'There's one obvious, very pointed, smaller mountain with a thumb-shape by its side, OK?' I continued. His faced was screwed up with concentration.

'I see it, Dad.' I checked to make sure that Kate was watching, too.

'Right, now behind that is a grey mountain that's triangular – a bit like this shape I'm making with my hands.' I put my fingers and thumbs together to form a point. 'It's got cloud blowing across it and off it.'

'I see it, the grey pointed thing,' Tom shouted exultantly, as one of the ridges of K2 filled the gap between the clouds. 'That's the second highest mountain in the world.'

I had fulfilled my promise to Tom and Kate twice now: they'd seen K2 both from the air through an aeroplane cockpit window and on the ground – not many miles away, either. As I spoke to them the curtains of cloud closed in again quickly. We had been granted a rare privilege – a view of K2 that very few people ever saw. We had the weather to thank for that. Someone, somewhere, obviously wanted us to see it.

It was unlikely that Alison, travelling in much worse weather than we were having, would have seen the mountain here. In the rain and floods her trekking party would have been forced to keep to a higher level where the views were a lot more restrictive. It took her eight days to get to base camp. I could just imagine how hard the going must have been on this boulder-strewn ground with 2 to 3 feet of fresh snow on it.

Thursday 22 June. Woke at 7.00 a.m. and realized how late it was and we had not been woken up to move. It snowed again in the night and I assume the porters were keen to dry out a little. They're amazing. They know we're going on a glacier and they have been issued with sunglasses and waterproof coats but they choose not to wear them. Instead, they stick to rubber plimsolls, no socks, the standard cotton Pakistani dress (shalwar qamis) with maybe just the addition of an odd scarf...Felt strong today and I was moving quickly. Enjoyed the walk, even though we had virtually no views. It was cold and kept trying to snow. After two hours we stopped and the kitchen boys set our cloth for a picnic in the snow! Another two hours' walking and we arrived at our designated camping spot...I moved some stones and pitched where it looked very clean. Another blizzard for half an hour.

It was incredible, I thought, as we wandered along back down towards the river Biaho Lungpa, that none of the so-called experts talking to the media had mentioned that K2 was visible on a good day just before you reach Paiju. Alison did not get her first view of K2 until she reached Concordia:

Saturday 24 June. Woke about 5.00 a.m. I knew we were not leaving until 6.30 a.m. but, even though I could have a lie-in, for some reason I unzipped the tent to look out – and wow – there was K2. I shouted 'I can see K2' in a singing voice, I was so happy. It was magnificent. As the clouds were rolling in, I decided to get straight up and get some photographs before it socked in. I got out of my tent, still inside my sleeping bag, and hopped about taking photographs.

We walked on to Paiju camp site around a sandy rock-strewn spur, a spot I had been looking forward to from the description in the guide books: '...the campsite at Paiju (3368 metres/11 050 feet)...is considered by many to be the best along the entire length of the trek. There is a good stream to wash in, green pastures, a grove of poplar trees and tremendous views' (*Lonely Planet Guide to Pakistan*).

The birch and poplar-lined gully system that defines the Paiju camp site certainly looked appealing on our approach but the camping terraces were a grave disappointment, filled with dirty sand and grit dust bowls. The area of flat ground behind the trees was completely barren and, when we arrived, covered in rubbish of all kinds. The site was terraced and the top tier had been taken over by some trekking organizations whose solution to the waste disposal problem was to simply pile it up in a big heap. Every time it rained all the nasty liquid residue washed down over our site into the stream. The hardly attractive or aesthetic toilet block actually added an air of dignity to an otherwise depressing sight. Ashraf was so upset by our attitude that he ordered the porters to pick up all the rubbish and to burn it or bury it. Despite having already completed a day's walk, they bent to the ground obediently. They did a wonderful job but it will take years for the grass and vegetation to grow back. There can be no justification for this type of careless destruction. I would like to see the site closed for five years and left to regenerate. It made me ashamed to be a climber, because it is they who do the damage with wanton disregard for the landscape they have supposedly come to experience. Even though the weather was perfect, none of us enjoyed staying there.

We all had an early night, but it was to be another fitful one for me. This time Kate woke a couple of times needing the loo. As I carried her over to the toilet block I could not help being dazzled by the beautiful starry night. There was my old friend Orion, complete with his belt and sword. Less than two months earlier I had sat on the cold step in front of my cottage in Scotland looking up at him, having just learnt of Alison's death. Here he was again, looking down on me halfway around the world, halfway between the last outposts of civilization and the mountain where she died.

Was I right to bring my children here? To me it was simple: I had made a promise to them, and here we were. They were quite used to their mum nipping off to climb mountains. She could be away a day, a week and, more recently, months, but to them time meant little. Two hours could feel like a lifetime for someone as young as Kate. She needed something concrete to understand that this time her mother was not coming home, otherwise Alison might have simply slipped out of her consciousness without Kate ever really coming to grips with what had happened. Tom, being older, understood enough to know that he wanted to mark her passing in some way. That was why he was so adamant about coming. To a young boy who has spent most of his life outdoors it seemed only fitting he should visit 'Mum's last mountain'; he had no idea of the distance or logistics involved when he made that request.

Before we left Britain our doctors, David and Cath, had some misgivings about making the journey with the children and spoke to one of Britain's top child psychiatrists, Dr Dora Black. She has conducted a great deal of research on grief in children which had shown benefit from promoting mourning. In general, remembering is helpful.

As our journey progressed, Cath fell into the role of bereavement counsellor for the children. She found the journey proved to be a trigger for both Tom and Kate to remember their mother and talk about her and, as importantly, to open up about her death. The image of K2 was a particularly strong one in Tom's psyche. Right from when we arrived in Islamabad, Cath, who kept a close professional and maternal eye on them, noticed that Tom was looking for a way to express himself. 'I felt he needed to communicate, in fact he gave me a sort of coded message that he'd written in imaginary Chinese on a serviette,' she told me. 'We were sitting down to dinner in the hotel when he nudged David and said, "That's for Cath". In blue felt-tip pen he had drawn a sort of mountain shape with this face on it and this indecipherable scribble around it. He wasn't prepared to talk about it at the time but I'm sure he was sort of saying to me that he really did want to talk about his mum and about her death.'

Cath had brought along work books specifically designed for children coming to terms with death and, occasionally, when there was a quiet moment in camp, she would lead Tom over to the mess tent where they would sit down together and go through them. Tom is quieter, introspective, more like his mother and less open about things than Kate and this seemed to be a way of allowing him to vent his pent-up feelings. By the time we reached Paiju he seemed able to talk more freely about what happened on the mountain and express his emotions quite openly*.

Of course, this was a trauma Alison had never intended her children to have to go through. Even in her most private moments she had never discussed the possibility of death. Whenever she was pressed in interviews, all she would say was that she 'enjoyed living too much'. The bodies of climbers frozen as they had fallen was a sight she had to expect on the major routes in the Himalayas. In her Everest diary she describes having to clamber over a corpse that had obviously been there for decades. When she was at K2 base camp she visited the grave of one of the twelve climbers who died on the mountain in the terrible year of 1986. In her diaries she described it as 'extremely sobering' but it did nothing to deter her from the climb. Alison never thought she would die, neither did anybody else. She had so much ability and when you saw her in the hills it was inconceivable that she could ever make a mistake. She probably didn't. That is the irony. She was caught by a freak of nature. Whether that was nature's way of reclaiming her I don't know, but Alison never put a foot wrong on a mountain.

*See Appendix I: A Doctor's Perspective by Cath Collier, page 193

CHAPTER ELEVEN

A SHORT WALK

'Why fear death? It is the most beautiful adventure in life.'
CHARLES FROHMAN

Noises from the mess tent signalled that tea was already on its way. Both Tom and Kate were fast asleep, so I slid quietly out of my bag, dressed and picked my way across camp for an early cuppa. As I drew level with the Collier's tent, a worried-looking Cath emerged. As she spoke, my eyes were drawn to the ground, which was sprinkled with toilet paper and crumpled paper tissues. 'David had a bad night – I think he has a serious problem with his stomach and gut,' she said. Knowing Cath as well as I did, I realized she was not one to be easily panicked. 'He has had almost continuous diarrhoea and sickness since the early hours. I also think he might have fractured his rib about three or four days ago because he took a nasty fall on the way up. He does feel absolutely terrible but the only good thing is I think the drugs I administered were absorbed by his stomach lining before he last threw up.'

It was clear we were going nowhere that day. Cath was sure from the start something serious was wrong with David and it was not just one of the usual vicious variations on 'Delhi Belly' or 'Kathmandu Quickstep'. David had been tucking into a dish of sheep's liver the evening before and she felt sure this had given him his dose of amoebic dysentery. However, her treatment was starting to work, albeit slowly. I popped over to see him and he almost looked human but it did not take a degree in medicine to realize that his race was run. Whilst we could leave David in situ, it did carry a major risk. I have never believed in splitting teams up: if one goes down, then everyone goes down. The problem was that at this altitude, 3368 metres

(11 050 feet), David would not recover at any sort of rate at all, and an illness like his could suddenly go from being uncomfortably bad to life-threatening. We were a long way from anywhere, although luckily we had some of the biggest toughest porters the Karakoram could provide so they could carry David out if necessary.

As the weather was perfect, we decided to let him rest at camp for the day and then see how he was later before we made any major decisions. We now had other pressing priorities. One was to get the surrounds of the Collier's tent cleared up and a second was to make it easier for David to reach the distant toilet block now that it was daylight. There was no way someone with chronic illness could manage a couple of hundred yards to the splendidly sited but slightly smelly squatter toilet over the next ridge. We decided to erect our portable 'Agincourt' privacy box – so-named because of its square turreted shape and bright yellow and pink stripes – for David's personal use. Suds unpacked one of our avalanche shovels, cleaned up the mess and took it over to the main rubbish pit for burning before burial. We were only just in time as David emerged from his tent and shot like a badly fired rocket into the tardis-like contraption.

Cath looked relieved when I told her of my decision; she clearly thought it was the correct one. Chris Terrill was a bit fazed, not being used to our strange mountain philosophies, but after a short while of toing and froing between our party and his team he accepted the picture.

I thought back to Saturday 24 June, the day I heard Alison had arrived at her base camp, just a month and eleven days since she had stood on the summit of Everest. Opportunities to join expeditions to these major mountains are few and far between, even for a climber of Alison's calibre. When this one came up for K2 she jumped at the chance, even though it was so soon after Everest, because she could not know if she would ever get one again. I think she secretly enjoyed the fact that it gave her the opportunity to escape all the pressure of media attention that had dominated the two weeks she was at home with us but, as ever, she hated to leave our children. She sent a fax to Scotland the day after she arrived at base camp.

Jim, How's things. We arrived at base camp yesterday after five days of bad weather. Now it is perfect but there are metres of fresh snow. Hope you and the children are well and that you all enjoy a great summer. Will keep you updated as possible. Could you please encourage Tom to read below.

Tom and Katie,
We have arrived at our base camp. The trek was difficult – it snowed every day. The mountain I have come to climb is called K2, it looks like this [there was a drawing below]. Be good for Daddy, have a lovely summer and enjoy your holiday.
With lots and lots of love from Mum.

Alison had been questioned time and again through the media about her role as a mother but I always believed she gave the children what she felt they needed and that was her love, affection, attention and a sense of value. Mothers, like anyone else, should have the freedom to do what they want to do and if that includes climbing mountains, driving racing cars, parachuting or any sport that's at the cutting edge of excitement, then they should do it. After all, how long is a mother a mother? Is it for the first three years, five years, fifteen years or twenty five years? So does that mean any woman, once she has had a baby, must then forgo anything to do with adventure? A fortnight before Alison died, two experienced British climbers were killed in the Haramosh range just a short way from where we were. They had both got children but it barely rated a mention. The fact that one had a six-year-old daughter didn't generate a great outcry that fathers shouldn't climb mountains. People don't seem to realize that women like Alison would not be the mothers, the partners or the wives they were if they were not able to fulfil the drive, the dreams and the expression of their talents.

Of course Alison was torn between the children and mountains, but a free spirit like hers needed to have both. Her last interview from K2 tries to imply she was thinking of giving up climbing altogether: '...because I'm so pissed off with the way things are going in climbing.

People have always been competitive, which I think is fine. But people are getting so dishonest about things and it pisses me off…At the moment I'm not sure whether I'll continue to be a 100 per cent professional climber' (the *Independent,* 2 September 1995). Even though I knew Alison for more than fifteen years, a great deal of this interview did not sound like her or ring particularly true. It should perhaps be pointed out that she agreed to conduct this interview with New Zealander Matt Comeskey for his local climbing magazine and was sharing her concerns specifically with others in the sport, even though it did end up in a British national newspaper.

Her diaries reveal some of the torment she was going through in her constant battle between the mountains and motherhood, but there is no suggestion that she had any intention of retiring from climbing. She might have wanted to retire from that expedition because of the atrocious conditions in the Himalayas – it is hard work climbing these super-giants without oxygen, without support, and without all the cosseting that happened in the old days with the larger expeditions. As Alison used to point out, every minute at high altitude your body is slowing dying because of the constant deprivation of oxygen, but I find it hard to imagine Alison ever giving up: climbing was too much a part of her.

Her diary comments have to be taken in the context of where she was and the fact she had been away from the children for over two months. She was fed up with the weather being so continually bad and frustrated by the fact that she had very nearly reached the summit earlier. She got to over 8000 metres (26 247 feet) alone, where she bivvied down for the night, but again the weather closed in and instead of pushing on to the top she came back down all the way to the bottom in one very long day.

K2 base camp, Wednesday 28 June. This year has gone by so quickly. I suppose I've achieved a fair amount, but I'm really missing Tom and Katie. It would be wonderful right now if I could pick them up and cuddle them. I would dearly love to stand on the summit of K2 but it would be wonderful

to be holding them, having fun with them and enjoying life together.
May God bless them and keep them safe and happy whilst I'm away.

K2 base camp, Monday 3 July. I've been missing Tom and Katie today
probably because I have had time to think about them. I've half felt like
not wanting really to stay and finish this 'job off' but — I don't know if
or when I'll get another chance, so I might regret it.

K2 base camp, Sunday 9 July. I would really love to be home by mid-
August. I am desperately missing Tom and Kate. Strangely enough I have
been dreaming about Derbyshire [where she grew up and where our
family home was until the end of 1992]. *I dream of days gardening*
and hiking with the children, the Derbyshire hills and holiday skiing. The
future is so undecided.

K2 base camp, Tuesday 11 July. July is whizzing away, which in some ways
is nice as it means the time to go home is drawing nearer — although the
time to summit is less. Today I rang Jim [by satellite phone]. *I really*
just want to cuddle Tom and Kate and be with them. I spoke for two and
a half minutes...I dream of Scotland and the children and to have a home
once more.

Alison never came home. Instead, I brought our children to her so
she could see them one last time. She had spent time with them in
some of the most beautiful and wildest places on God's earth. She
had seen them growing up where every child should have the
opportunity to grow up — in the wide open spaces, in freedom, having
adventures and learning to look after themselves in a natural way. If
there is anything sad at all about Alison's death, it is the fact that she
can never see her children grow up. That's all. For the rest, there is
no sadness; she was where she had to be and where she wanted to be,
as her diary explains:

K2 base camp, Saturday 5 August. The porters are here and I am to leave
tomorrow morning. Climbing K2 is very important to me but I can't keep

*waiting and waiting. I've been here six weeks now and had a few tries –
twice to camp 3 and once to camp 4 – the weather each time has shut me
down – it is obviously not to be. Tom goes back to school soon – I'd like
some time with him. They're young and time flies by – I want – I feel I
should be with them.*

*Maybe I've failed here, I've worked hard but somehow it's not come
together. Yesterday I was in tears coming down the strip* [climbers' slang
for the base-camp area] *– exhausted, mentally and physically. I've put
in so much but somehow it's not to be. I am feeling however, pressure back
home – 'why' I failed, what went wrong. Personally it doesn't matter but I
worry how everyone else will see it. It will take a long time to analyse and
weigh it up.*

*It eats away at me – wanting the children and wanting K2 – I feel
like I'm being pulled in two. Maybe they'd be happier if Mum was around
but maybe summiting K2 would help me make a better future for them.
Long term having me back safe and sound is surely more important?*

*K2 base camp, Sunday 6 August. Oh well, it's 10.30 a.m. and I'm still
here at K2 base camp – last night I couldn't sleep – I was worried I had
made the wrong decision – I didn't feel I could walk away from here
leaving Rob* [Slater] *and the Kiwis* [Peter Hillary's New Zealand
expedition] *to try again, I had to stay and try once more too. I kept
unzipping the tent last night to look at the weather. It really didn't look
too bad. I had to stay and try again…I feel like a lead weight has gone
from my shoulders. I'm sitting here with the Kiwis – I'm happy my
decision is the right one…I feel much more content, restful and happier
now – I have a job to do and will try my best to do it.*

*K2 base camp, Monday 7 August. I've come such a long way and put in
so much physically and mentally. Surely a couple of weeks really won't
make any difference?*

Back home in Scotland, Tom, Kate and I had been enjoying glorious
summer weather, making daily trips to the beach and exploring the area

around our new Scottish home. I had written to Alison on 14 August:

Dear Alison

It has been an amazing summer since you went out to K2. The weather has been mostly blue skies and sunshine, day in, day out…Of course, we would all have loved to have you with us in this special summer but Tom and Kate realize that this time they had to stay at home and time has passed quickly with all our action. They will be able to show you all the new sites if Scotland has an Indian summer…I am sure that your decision to acclimatize slowly was the right one – of course you should sit out the bad weather as long as you can. Look after yourself and come home safe.

Again Tom and Kate had added their distinctive scrawl to the bottom. Two days later I heard Alison was dead. When I wrote the letter she had already been killed, blown off the mountain top by an unexpected jet wind.

K2 base camp, Wednesday 9 August. Rob [Slater] went past at 9.00 a.m. excited – the weather was improving and as he said 'We must go tomorrow'. There were some patches of blue sky – no mist, but a lot of clouds racing by. The wind has definitely changed direction – but unfortunately to the north. Throughout the morning K2 looked progressively better and better – huge plumes of cloud indicated high winds – but at least the weather was on the move.

Everyone has been in high spirits all day. The Spanish who have porters coming on the 14th and leaving on the 15th said that if the weather hadn't cleared by the 10th they couldn't try for the summit. A day of sun today – the 9th – has boosted their optimism.

The sunset is fantastic, pink on Chogolisa, Broad Peak and K2 – we don't really know what the weather is doing but hope it holds for long enough. We've ordered porters to take us to Hushe leaving here on the 16th – so will have one last try before then. There's still banks of clouds

*behind Chogolisa — but the rest of the sky is clear. Can we possibly be
offered the chance to summit? God willing.*

This was the last entry in Alison's diary.

CHAPTER TWELVE

A PROMISE MADE

'The most important thing in living is to reach out
and touch perfection in that which they most loved to do.'

FROM *JONATHAN LIVINGSTON SEAGULL*
BY RICHARD BACH

If nature intended Tom and Kate to see K2 from the ground in the same season that their mother died, then it would happen; if not, then that was the way it was meant to be. It was 6 October and the weather was absolutely perfect – clear, azure-blue sky, no clouds and just the hint of.a cooling breeze. The whole area in towards the mountain was empty. It was Friday, the holy day in the Muslim week, so it looked as though we would have the area beyond Paiju completely to ourselves.

I wanted to walk for an hour towards the Baltoro glacier and then traverse into a position on a suitable ridge where the children could see clearly K2 and the particular summit area where Alison had so successfully stood on that fateful day, Sunday 13 August 1995 – three calendar months to the day after she sat on the highest point on earth.

David, still out of action, remained in his sleeping bag but the rest of us set off. No-one spoke much and even Tom and Kate were silent. They could sense this was an important moment for all of us. The only sound was the scrunching of boots on sandy gravel and the occasional clunk as a foot kicked a stone against another. We were awed by the plain simple beauty of the place; it was so inspiring, so dominating and challenging. This was the landscape that Alison belonged to and now it belonged to Alison. For the first time since we set off I could sense her spirit, wild and free. The air was so clear, so transparent, that you felt you could simply reach out and touch the surrounding mountains. The bone-white streaks of salt that made up the strange landscape are what gave the Paiju area its name. The saline deposits broke up the mustards and browns that colour the high-altitude desert hillside. The usual scrub bushes and herb-type plants gave way to more rocky fare but, occasionally, as someone trod or brushed against this low hardy vegetation, a wonderful spicy, clean fragrance would drift past your nose.

I don't think any of us will forget the walk. It lasted only sixty minutes but every mountain stood out in perfect light. Even the porters, who must pass through there almost weekly each season, were absorbed by the atmosphere. Ashraf had sensed the sombre nature of the occasion and understood this was the point where the children would say their final goodbyes. Without informing myself or anyone else he had selected only his key senior Hushe men to accompany us on this last, short journey. They did so without ceremony or fuss but with pride because of what it meant. They had taken Tom and Kate to their hearts and understood the loss that had brought them to this remote and wonderful place. As we walked the gentle breeze carried with it the scent of wild lavender, even though there was no sign of the plants around us.

I looked at my watch and even that triggered happy memories. A misty Welsh morning in Llandberis pass. Watching over Kate, still a baby, asleep in a down jacket while I read. 'Dad, Dad.' Tom's eager call came from the nearby stream. He scrambled up the bank. 'I have found a clock.' I put down the book I was engrossed in, checked a tiny Kate was still snoring and jumped down through the boulders to where Tom had been playing with his smart plastic fire tug in a clear pool. There, almost filling his small palm, was a wrist watch without a strap. Later, Alison took it to a watch repairer she knew in her old home town of Belper in Derbyshire and, with a new battery inside, away it went. Now it sat on my wrist with a faded purple nylon and Velcro strap that Alison had been given. It had kept perfect time for us throughout the trip. Strangely, as I looked at it, I sensed all would be fine and dandy.

Great Trango, washed in ochre, red and brown with vivid streaks of purest white snow, looked like a fantasy castle from Arthurian legend. This was just left of centre stage in our mountain vista. Further left still was a host of almost black granite triangles. Towards the right was a particularly attractive isosceles triangle-shaped peak that had on its immediate right-hand side a deep notch with a beckoning finger of rock stark against the drum of ice of the Savoie range. Then there was K2. It stood dominant and overpowering behind the others. A pyramid of white flecked with steel-grey rock, black shadows and the odd tawny hollow. I stood and stared. It ought to be the highest mountain on earth. Everest has the sheer bulk to impress but K2 is the mountain that rises most dramatically above its surrounding peaks. It almost taunts humanity to defy its raw, untamed power. I had never seen a mountain that could command such respect from afar. Alison had reached its summit.

I saw her smiling face in front of me, that distinctive smile that went from the top of one ear to the other. I saw it coming out of the darkness when she'd climbed the Shroud on the Grande Jorasse in 1993, having walked all the way from the valley and back. She had finally got the first of the Big Six under her belt after nearly four months of dreadful weather. That was her moment, a challenge fulfilled. That was Alison the Climber: strong, independent and so, so talented. My mind switched to another memory, softer but more poignant, of later that same night. The showers were off and she was desperately sweaty and shivering with cold so I got buckets of hot water out of the hand sinks and, as she stood naked in the middle of the public camp site (it was in the early hours of the morning), poured them over her, before dressing her in every piece of fleece we had and slotting her into a sleeping bag. She was the young girl again, tired and needing to be looked after. All she wanted was a warm place to sleep, her great achievement forgotten, at least until the morning.

I had never been quite happy inside about having the children commit their private ceremony, their farewell to their mother, in public up on the Baltoro glacier. But the BBC team themselves decided to film only with their longest lenses from as far away as was practical. There was no feeling of an insensitive prying glass eye. Chris Terrill was finding it hard to hold himself together. I knew he was finding the scene incredibly difficult because he himself had just lost a dearly loved niece in a swimming-pool accident in America. He had not been able to go and comfort his sister because he had been contracted to do this trip.

Tom and I were up ahead of the others on the crest of brown rock that was the last high ground of solid mother earth before we scrambled onto the rock and ice of the retreating Baltoro glacier. I had imagined the scene in my head but now it felt as if we had been here before, even though none of us ever had. That was what was so strange. It was not until I read Alison's recovered diaries that I realized she too had crossed this rough rocky terrain and been touched by this very spot.

> *Tuesday 20 June. Soon onto the Baltoro glacier. Some tremendous views of Great Trango. What an impressive range of rocky mountains. When the light was right – the golden granite was beautiful – contrasted by the crystal-blue sky. At the end of the glacier the path was diverted around an enormous crevasse...An amazing place, silt mud and sand from the glacier to our right – a broken mass of grey ice crags and black broken rocks. I walked across the mud and silt and marvelled at the amazing forms and shapes of nature's ways.*

The ridge and rib we were on sloped and curled down to a yawning mouth of black ice, from which a stream issued at the start of the waters that drain the K2 massif. Gently Tom and I turned and kept to the very crest, the spine, the backbone and gravitated to The Spot. We knew where was right. The words from Pink Floyd's 'Wish You Were Here'* came to me:

> So, so you think you can tell Heaven from Hell,
> blue skies from pain.

*Written by Roger Waters

Can you tell a green field from a cold steel rail?
A smile from a veil?
Do you think you can tell?

We knew we were as far as we needed to travel. The Balti team, those hard nut-brown men of the mountains, sat ankles crossed at the back in an arc. None of them said a word as Tom, Kate and I walked forward.

I knew the kind of farewell Alison wanted. I remembered Rupert, our Border collie she had loved so dearly and from whom she had become inseparable. The day he died at fifteen years old was a sad one and we decided that he needed a special send-off. With tears flowing, I had dug a large deep hole in the orchard at the end of our garden in Derbyshire and we buried him with all his possessions and food for the onward journey to Valhalla. A true Viking funeral for a true Viking dog. This was my way of arranging for Alison to have the same in spirit, even if her body had been kept by the mountain.

Alison had really taken to Tibet on her travels there and while in Lhasa she had bought some Chinese silk flowers. One of these she had left at the summit of Everest; another she had carried with her to K2. It may even now be tucked under the snow on this savage mountain's peak. The rest of the flowers I put in an empty wine bottle with a pleasing shape and they found a place adorning the breakfast room in our Scottish cottage in the Great Glen. I had brought a selection of these flowers with us so that, along with the personal drawings by Tom and Kate, the children could leave them as part of the final 'au revoir' to their mother. I had the silk flowers in my hand. Tom and Kate chose their own memorial, their own talismans. Tom started his preparations. I did not tell him what to do, instinct guided him. He had played in terrain like this many times before with his mother. This time is was for his mother, who had been taken by these very beautiful mountains and the most fundamental of elements, wind and ice. Tom's small hands brushed the sandy soil flat and he laid out his favourite K2 drawing and held it in place with four flat rocks. The flower was laid diagonally, corner to corner. I sat on top of a boulder and watched him. I felt confident that no-one would ever identify this exact location again. It was Tom, Kate and Alison's cathedral with K2 at the far end, like an untouchable altar. It was no-one else's, not even mine. This was the end of my simple promise.

I talked to both Tom and Kate — I have no idea what about. As we talked, Tom gathered stones and started to build his cairn. Kate, the young sister, was not going to be left out. She grabbed her smaller, but still precious drawing and, imitating Tom, carefully assembled a similar little monument to her mother just slightly smaller than his, which seemed somehow fitting.

I risked a look over my shoulder. The Baltis were cast in stone, the strong sunlight turning their dark, sun-tanned faces to jet-black masks. Suds was there, just watching, not a movement, like the Scottish mountains he had grown up in — solid, dependable and oh so honest. Yes, Alison would be enjoying this. She would be wondering where the great shambling bear David was, but he was here in spirit by force of will alone. Cath, the Welsh sprite, was darting around, cameras around her neck; Cally, always an elusive girl, was way off somewhere lost in her own thoughts and memories. She and I had shared the triumph of Everest from Scotland as well as the tragedy of K2. We had dealt with the press and public that inundated Nevis Range when news of Alison's success on Everest was broken.

I shall never forget the day Alison returned from that record-breaking ascent. The whole world seemed to have descended on Scotland as she sat there surrounded by reporters and television film crews in the alpine-style Snowgoose restaurant halfway up Aonach Mor at the Nevis Range ski centre. She had finished posing for photographs and was about to start a press conference but she managed to sneak away for a moment's peace into a back room with Tom and Kate. As our daughter climbed onto her knee and our son burrowed his way under her arm, all thoughts of mountains and media were gone. She was just a mother, relaxed and at ease. The press pack eventually drew her back but even then she wanted her children near. Tom became bored and wandered away but Kate stayed with her mother. As Alison signed books and T-shirts Kate played at adding her own scribble underneath. Alison admitted then that climbing Everest had been the happiest day in her climbing life.

Tom came back with more stones than Kate could carry. I unfolded my stiff knee joints and went to help them. Tom wanted to do most of it on his own but, as usual, Kate took all the help she could get. The cairns, about 5 or 6 feet apart, began to take shape. Tom's quickly gained height as he had more building skill than his sister; Kate's was more of a pyramid that crudely aped the shape of the mountain before us.

And did they get you to trade your heroes for ghosts?
Hot ashes for trees?
Hot air for a cool breeze?
Cold comfort for change?
And did you exchange a walk on part in a war
for a lead role in a cage?

The tiny stones were flat-sided, just the right sort of nature's building bricks for small fingers. Tom walked away and looked; he was satisfied with his efforts but did not smile. He knew why he had made it and that filled him with sadness. For Kate, only the simple but very concrete sight of her mother's last mountain seemed to be an image she could understand. The rest was a game with the added bonus of an audience, which she always liked. She looked round and spotted Ashraf and his boys unpacking some food, local mountain produce that they had carefully held back for this moment: dried apricots, the traditional fruit of the region; almonds, small but delicious; raisins and mulberries — all foods that the locals believe aid living at these heights. She dropped her remaining stones, wandered over to them and picked up some of the delicacies. Tom was not going to be left out and he followed her over, only to return to his cairn with his hands full of the rich autumnal fruits. He popped a few into his mouth then filled in the small gaps between the stones with the nuts and the apricots.

How I wish, how I wish you were here.
We're just two lost souls swimming in a fish bowl, year after year,
Running over the same old ground. What have we found?
The same old fears.
Wish you were here.

Kate decided that she, too, would leave some food for her mother. Alison must have smiled at this, those brown eyes lighting up that wide brow and gently arching eyebrows as she looked down at the two people most dear to her paying tribute in the best way they could. Children have a great natural sense of timing. Kate decided she had finished, picked herself up and went looking for Cath. Tom watched her go but walked around his cairn then sat down and looked at K2, his little figure dwarfed by many of the boulders littering this glacial area. There were no tears, no hysterics, just quiet, thoughtful contemplation, a last moment with his mother. Slowly, he pulled himself to his feet and wandered to where I stood. It was his way of telling me it was time to say goodbye. Time to start back and get on with our new, different life.

You don't have to wear your feelings on your arm to have real feelings; it is what you think inside and how you live your life that shows your worth. I said my final goodbye to Alison on the Wednesday after she died when the hairs stood up on the back of my neck and I knew she was dead. I said my 'au revoir' in the dark just before dawn on Thursday morning. We never said goodbye at stations, never said goodbye at the bottom of routes, never said goodbye when we parted. Only now was it appropriate. My philosophy has always been that you have to accept what life has for you. Alison died where she wanted to be, doing what she wanted. I was just thankful it was not a futile death, like a car accident or a drawn-out disease, which are the real tragedies. That Sunday closed my life with Alison. I brought my children here so she could have one last look at them. Even for the children this was the last page in their chapter with their mother. A new page awaited and it was up to them to write on it. I would do my best to let them live their lives in a stylish and adventurous way that gave them pleasure and fulfilment. It was time to go. We turned and slowly walked back over the rocks and scree.

The spell was broken and the BBC moved in for an interview. I avoided looking into the staring glass lens and instead found Chris Terrill's liquid eyes. Only willpower was holding back his tears. The questions were gentle but necessary. He had simple notes. He held my gaze for one last, big effort. 'Would it be fair to say,' he asked, 'that Alison could be compared to the fallen in war?' He quoted 'For the Fallen' by Laurence Binyon:

> They shall grow not old, as we that are left grow old:
> Age shall not weary them, nor the years condemn.
> At the going down of the sun and in the morning
> We will remember them.

It was time for all of us to raise our hats and salute. The film crew started to pack. Chris broke ranks and, without a word, shot off into the near distance and stood still, rock-like, looking at K2. Then he bent and built his own cairn. At last he had wrenched his sister's and his own grief for the death of his niece out of his head. It had been hard and painful to watch but I felt pleased for him. He walked back and stood by me, shoulder to shoulder. My arm automatically went around him and I gave him a hug. It seemed the right thing to do. 'It is so beautiful, I think I understand, I think I know...' was all he said, all he needed to say. He understood why people climb mountains, whether they are the real ones of rock, ice and snow or just the mountains of everyday life. They are the hard ones to keep on trying.

CHAPTER THIRTEEN

A PROMISE KEPT

'There are no graves here. These mountains and
plains are a cradle and a stepping stone...
look well thereupon and you shall see yourselves
and your children dancing hand in hand.'

KAHIL GIBRAN

The sun was hot as we turned our backs on K2. The air was so still and clear that you could see the dust kicked up by Ashraf and the Hushe boys a little way ahead of us as we trekked quietly back towards Paiju. As my heavily booted feet crunched over stones and rocks and down through slippery scree, a thousand images of Alison filled my head.

The years slipped away as I pictured that small, serious and thoughtful girl behind the counter taking in every word uttered by the rock climbers who came into the shop. Alison worked for my company as a Saturday girl in one of our climbing stores in Matlock Bath, Derbyshire, from the age of eighteen. Even then, I knew there was more to her than met the eye. Like everyone else I had heard the rumour going around the Peak District climbing grapevine about the young girl who did not find anything particularly difficult and was totally committed to the sport. On Saturdays she would always arrive for work bang on time and, instead of collecting her wages every week, she would put them towards buying an item from the shop.

I had a long-standing engagement to be a guest at a climbing club dinner and, as I had separated from my wife a few months earlier, I thought of Alison because it gave her another entry into the (then) extremely male-dominated climbing world. At that time it was very difficult for women, and even more so young girls, to meet other climbers because most clubs met in pubs over copious pints of bitter and were considered no place for a woman – particularly a petite, slim brunette – even if she could already climb better than most of them put together. In fact, I think that was part of the trouble. Alison's male counterparts were always the first to voice their cynicism about her achievements and it did not stop when she became successful. The knockers always claimed she only got good sponsorship deals because she was a woman and received the media attention purely because she was a mother of two young children. This was just that green-eyed monster jealousy talking. It happens in every walk of life and particularly to women achievers and has, I think, something to do with the male ego feeling bruised and basic age-old sexual discrimination. Anyway, I invited Alison along to the climbing club dinner and we hit it off. We went rock climbing together the next day and a few times after that. Gradually we realized we had something more in common than just a love of rock and mountains. It just seemed apparent that we were to spend at least part of our life on this earth together. She came to live with me on her eighteenth birthday.

Despite rebelling against her parents' wishes – they did not approve of her moving in and abandoning their plans for her to go to Oxford – Alison was not a maverick like me. She had a classic middle-class, middle England upbringing in Derbyshire and preferred to stick firmly to those attitudes. However, she did need somebody very strong to share her life with. Throughout my forty-nine years any relationship I have had has been with people who, at their simplest, are interesting – people who can make you realize that there is more to life than just accepting the status quo. Living with a climbing genius, which I believe Alison was, wasn't easy. She was incredibly strong-willed, as I am, incredibly stubborn, which I'm not – I just get to where I want to go in a different way – and she could be very highly strung. When her head went into gear it was easier trying to bend stainless steel bars in your teeth than to get Alison to move, but that is how it has to be if you want to achieve what she did.

I believed in Alison's climbing talent from the start and knew I had to do whatever was within my capabilities to nourish it and allow her to develop. She would have been a success whatever route she took because her talent was so awesome. If she had not met me she would probably have followed the usual career path chosen by those passionate about outdoor sports. She may have gone into teaching, where you get long holidays and can pursue a time-consuming obsession like climbing, or she might have worked in an outdoor centre; either way it would have taken her a lot longer to arrive at the very highest levels. Living with me did mean that she could always climb when she wanted to.

As far as Alison was concerned her profession was climbing. She went off to work and, if you like, her office or factory was K2, or Everest, or whichever mountain she was climbing at the time. That is what fed the family. The sponsorship deals to wear and test clothing, footwear, rucksacks, sleeping bags, tents and ropes were the things that paid for us to live our modest lifestyle. The books, the lectures and the sale of our photographs were the things that put jam on the bread or cheese on the pasta. In professional climbing such monetary rewards are relatively small beer compared to, say, the amounts earned in really high-profile sports such as tennis, golf or snooker, but they did allow Alison and the family a lifestyle that gave us the pleasure and freedom to continue climbing. Of course, it meant Alison and I had to cooperate in ways that other people often don't have to. There were times when you had to forget that you were husband and wife and switch into professional mode. If I was doing her publicity or an advertising photo shoot, I would work with Alison as a model like anyone else. When we went to the mountains the children just accepted that they too would sometimes have to be photographed by the media. It was all part of the job.

I never really believed Alison would actually die on a mountain and I found my own thoughts about her death far more complex than I had imagined. After the news broke I had the best part of a night and morning to decide how to face the world and Alison's death – or as it was then, likely death – on K2. In the end I decided I could only be myself. I didn't break down in public as everyone seemed to expect because that is not my way. Anyone from Yorkshire would understand that. One of the things that my generation suffered from, especially being brought up in the north of England, is that people didn't talk enough. They were very honest, but tended to keep most of their real feelings to themselves. I know my own family was very much like that. As a family unit, Alison and I always believed we should be as honest with our children as we could, at least in terms that they would understand. After Alison's death the only people I shared my emotions with were Tom and Kate.

However, the hundreds of letters of condolence that we received did affect me deeply. One that I found particularly hard to cope with was from the family of Dan Eldon, the twenty-three-year-old photographer killed in Mogadishu after achieving fame for his pictures on the front cover of magazines like *Time* and *Newsweek*. His sister, Amy, drew a picture of a mountain with the children and me on one side and her on the other, and then clouds with people on them. It was addressed to Tom and Kate and told them not to worry because her brother had gone before to prepare things for their mum. It took me almost a week before I could finish reading it, it was so simple and beautiful. The ideas expressed there still affect me even now.

I don't want to see K2 as Alison's grave. I have never subscribed to the belief that life just ends with the flesh – life's about spirit. I cannot believe someone with Alison's drive, sense of adventure and determination ends just like that. If there is a celestial place up there, then no doubt Alison has put together a dream team from all her climbing heroes who passed on before – Dougal Haston (1940–77), Hermann Buhl (1924–57) and Alan Rouse (1951–86) – and will be off tackling all those mountains that nobody has time in life to do.

The scuffle of soft footsteps behind me became louder and a small, hot hand slipped into mine. Tom and I walked hand in hand back to Paiju. When we arrived, the place was hardly recognizable from the rubbish heap we had seen the afternoon before. Ashraf had

had the porters working again, burning all they could and burying the rest. Our cook, Little Ibrahim, saw us coming and got his assistants to fire the stoves into life for a much-needed throat quencher, while Cath went over to her tent to see if David was on the mend. She had dished out some powerful antibiotics before we left and at last he seemed to be spending more time recuperating in bed than in his pink-and-yellow toilet extension.

Ever since we set off from Askoli we had been accompanied by a pair of shaggy sheep and a scrawny goat that had trotted submissively alongside the porters wherever they went. Paiju was to be the end of the road for these creatures – they were the porters' bonus. Mutton stew would be had around the camp fires that evening, along with the usual salt tea and Balti bread. The porters were in high spirits, anticipating their well-deserved treat.

Once again it was the Hushe boys who led the beasts away down the hillside to be slaughtered. Normally they would carry out the ceremony at camp but with so many vegetarians around they were afraid this would cause offence. Ever conscious of the sensitivities of their two young wards they did it out of sight and as unobtrusively as possible. It still did not make me feel much better about it, but I was a guest in their country and that was how things were done. In no time at all they were back with the sheep dispatched, skinned and ready for cooking. The porters all gathered in a rough circle around the Hushe camping area, which was on the left bank and, of course, occupied the choice top terrace, sheltered by trees, below us. A dirty grey sheet was spread on to the bare earth and the bloody carcasses were laid out as a particularly fiercesome-looking Hushe – yet another cousin of Ibrahim's – bent down, pushed his nating to the back of his head and ran a gnarled and dirty thumb along the edge of his rusty meat cleaver. Down it came with a bone-splitting thud, time and time again, until he and those close to him were spattered with bits of flesh and blood. The pieces of meat were cut and recut until the portions had been divided into 250-gram (just over half a pound) steaks, all without the use of scales. Much advice and comment was shouted by the waiting hungry hordes and, looking down from our terrace onto this circus, it was hard to believe that we had only brought eighty porters with us.

At last it was distribution time. Cath heaved a sigh of relief when the cleaver was put away without her sewing skills being required. The porters moved in to pick up their chosen portions. Old tins were filled with water taken directly from the stream and fires all over the hillside were blown into life for tea and stew. In this hard, basic economy as soon as you got a food bonus you ate it; you certainly could not stick it in the freezer or take it home with you.

It was such a pleasant afternoon with a powerful sun and the clearest of blue skies that Cally and Cath took Tom and Kate down to the river for a splash and the rest of the team soon joined them, with the exception of dear old David of course. I got on with some writing and, as expedition leader, discussed with Ashraf the best way to split up our team so that the BBC had plenty of good, strong, reliable porters. Earlier, Chris Terrill had gone into one of his powerful directorial moods and announced that he and his lads needed to push on the next day and film K2 from Concordia so that he would have all the necessary images to hand when he edited the film. Despite my former reservations, I decided to part with the BBC boys and take the rest of the team back to Tongol and the jeep road and wait for them there. They would be in good hands.

David was very weak and, as the children had seen their mum's last mountain on a fabulous day, my decision stood. We would head slowly back down the valley, leaving in the morning and strolling out in short stages. David's large build would not have been fun to carry over such demanding terrain. We could, of course, have sent a runner or, if we got desperate, used the satellite phone to summon up a rescue helicopter, but that would have caused real problems as Cath would have wanted to fly out too, which would have left Tom and Kate without any medical back-up. As we had an early start, I had a quick ice-cold foot wash in the stream, then it was early supper and bed for all.

I popped my head out of the tent at dawn and noted that the Colliers seemed quiet. Things looked promising. I pulled myself out and joined Sudsy for our usual early morning cup of tea and within minutes Cath, who must have heard us, was making her way across. Her drugs had done the business and David was weak but confident that if he carried nothing and kept a slow, steady pace, he would be able to go today. The other porters packed quickly and almost before breakfast was over we were shaking hands with El Tel, aka Chris Terrill. David, pale and drawn, set off before us. Every footstep must have felt like torture but he managed to keep up a steady totter. Suds, Cath, Cally and I followed closely behind for moral support. We did not look back or stop but picked our way slowly and carefully along the narrow track as it unwound across the hillside until we were under the centre of the Paiju peak itself. On our way in, this towering slab of rock and ice had been coy and mysterious, wreathed in mist and low cloud, but now it was sunlit in all its glory. A fine straw-coloured granite arrowhead topped a slender selection of high narrow ribs that met near the summit. It looked a fine climbing peak for 'rock jocks', as such specialists are mockingly known. The left side was well seen and even from our vantage point the receding steel-grey glacier and the polished steep granite approach looked hard. David slowed as we picked our way across a huge field of scree, over rocks and boulders coloured gold to rust-red with the aromatic scrub once again enveloping us in its fragrance.

Our porters had all shot ahead and were just visible as black dots gathering on a far-off ridge. This was where the boulders were at their largest and a fair-sized river ran across the ridge side of a shallow valley. Pockets full of crystal formations glittered in the rock and the younger and more energetic porters were off hunting for the sparkling minerals by the time we arrived. The cooks had set chairs out for us with barrels as tables for our lunch and all the seats were arranged so that you could not in any way help but look onto K2. The weather was not quite so sunny or as perfectly clear as before, but it was still an almost unbelievable view.

This was the very last real view of K2 we would have and once again the pyramid was clearly etched on the horizon. My attention was suddenly snatched away as I noticed Kate, who had climbed down off Ibrahim, sitting on the ground running sandy soil through her fingers and onto her lap. 'Get off the floor, please, Kate – you will get filthy dirty,' I demanded. Reluctantly, she did as she was told and dawdled bad-temperedly back towards her minder. The cooks packed up the stoves and we put away our cameras and swung rucksacks onto our shoulders once more. As we made our last adieu to the mountain, a wind-blown spume of powdery snow flew from the side of the summit. It looked for all the world just like a white silk handkerchief. Was it too fanciful to say it was Alison, waving her last goodbye to her much-loved children? The one certainty was that her spirit was free, as free as the wind, alive in that cold world of ice, rock and snow. A rare air for a rare talent to play in. Another Pink Floyd favourite track, 'Comfortably Numb'*, slipped into my head:

> There is no pain, you are receding
> A distant ship smoke on the horizon
> You are only coming through in waves
> Your lips move but I can't hear what you are saying.

*Written by Roger Waters

CHAPTER FOURTEEN

HOMEWARD BOUND

'The springs of enchantment lie within ourselves:
they arise from our sense of wonder, that most precious
of gifts, the birthright of every child.'

ERIC SHIPTON

I felt a persistent tug at my sleeve. 'Dad, do you want some of our bread?' Tom was standing at my side with Kate peeping over his shoulder. I looked down and there in his hands were two very neatly sculpted discs of muddy silt. It was baking night for the porters again and Tom and Kate had decided to rustle up their own version of Balti bread. I had not noticed Tom and Kate find their own stone-wall shelter and create their own imaginary fire earlier as I had been lured over to the real thing by the smell of fresh baking wafting in my direction. The children had obviously been watching and copying the porters, energetically kneading and pummelling their piles of muddy soil into the right shape. I felt proud of them – it showed they were taking in what was going on around them and absorbing this distinctive lifestyle. Forget books or even photographs, there can be no better way for two young children to gain an understanding of another culture than by watching it unfold at first hand. I picked one of the muddy rounds being offered to me by Tom and pretended to take a mouthful. 'Delicious, Tom. I hope we are going to have some for supper?' I said, joining in his game.

'In that case I had better go and make some more – come on Kate,' he chirped, and off they scurried to their little lair to continue their mud-pie making, much to the amusement of the Hushe boys.

We were camping at Gambo Chou for the night, where we had

also stayed on our way in. The gentle cooking ritual helped me relax; it had been a stressful day watching David struggle along not knowing whether he was going to improve or deteriorate and recognizing that responsibility for him and the rest of the team lay with me. I was glad our journey in had gone smoothly, but I almost felt that the pressure now was stronger than ever. I could not let anything go wrong on the way back and urged myself not to get too complacent. There were still some major obstacles ahead: one was the re-crossing of the precarious Flying Fox cable bridge; then there was the Biafo glacier and the high traverse around the rock buttress just before we reached Askoli. During our walk I knew Kate was in safe hands with Ibrahim but my eyes continually returned to Tom and David to make sure neither of them were flagging.

I had a fitful night. Even though my own common sense told me otherwise, the comments made in the media about the dangers for the children continued to echo. I knew that if the slightest thing went wrong I faced a lynch mob when I returned home. Sadly, this forced me to turn what should have been a roller coaster voyage of discovery into a controlled adventure, which is never as good.

The sight of sunshine streaming through the open tent door the next morning helped put my mind at ease but as I sat perched on a barrel outside the mess tent sipping my usual morning tea, a pale and sickly apparition materialized before me, immediately sparking new concerns. It was Cath and she looked like death. She gave me a weak smile. 'God, you look awful, lass,' I cried, jumping up and helping her to her seat.

'I know, I had a pretty bad night but I think I am OK today,' she replied in a hoarse voice. I had my doubts. Sharing a tent with David she had inevitably picked up amoebic dysentery as well, albeit in a milder form. I recalled our trip to Everest base camp when Cath and I had both succumbed to giardia at the same time and remembered how resilient she had been. On that occasion she had torn herself from her sick-bed when it was time to start the trek because she did not want to let the rest of us down: I sensed she should really have been tucked up in a sleeping bag now but I knew once her determined Celtic mind was made up there was no swaying her. Instead I sat quietly while she swallowed cups of hot black tea and pushed away the chapattis and jam placed before her. At least when David appeared a few minutes later he appeared to be on the mend, even managing some fried eggs for breakfast. His concerns were now for his wife and I could understand why.

I could not help sensing the irony in the fact both our doctors had fallen ill, although it was no joking matter. Even 'iron man' Sudsy was beginning to feel a little queasy after indulging in a night's feasting on mutton with the Hushe boys. (Sudsy more than anyone had hit it off with these hardy mountain folk, particularly Ashraf. The pair were cut from the same cloth, despite living half a world away.) Our pace was slow as we set off for another day's trek. Neither David nor Cath were up to much strenuous exertion and, as we would have to wait for the BBC to catch up with us at Tongol, there was no hurry. I was also worried that Tom and Kate might be the next candidates for the disease as they had spent many happy hours playing with Cath over the last few days. So far, neither was showing any signs of ill health but all I could do was make sure their hands were scrupulously clean before and after they ate anything. As usual, Tom strode off in front of me, ski poles in hand.

Now it was Cally's turn to sidle up to me with her own dilemma. I knew before we left Scotland that she had bowed out of her older sister's wedding to come on the trip, causing a sibling rift in the process. However, she had promised that if it was in any way possible, she would make every effort to get back to Scotland in time. The wedding was now less than a week away and the possibility of going on ahead when we neared civilization was mooted. 'Do you have any objections?' she enquired tentatively.

'Do what you want to do, but you know that I don't think you should break up a team on a trip like this,' I replied tersely, snapping, 'Maybe you shouldn't have come at all if you knew you would not see it through.' My temper quickly burnt itself out and I calmed down, recognizing Cally's dilemma. We consulted Ashraf. 'Well, Mr James, if she wants to go with one of my porters we should be able to get her to Tongol where she could catch a cargo jeep out,' he said, although he could offer no guarantees they could get there in time. Even if she reached Skardu on schedule, she would still have a flight back to Islamabad, then one to England and another to Scotland. Cally decided to take the gamble but we left it that she would stay with the rest of us until after we had crossed the treacherous Biafo glacier the following day.

That night was spent at Branchin in the shadow of the prominent rock buttress running down from the Bakhor Das peak. Our tents were pitched in a straight line along the top of a small cliff and, as David was by this point feeling much better, he spent the evening with the children making dams and sand castles down by the water, much to Tom and Kate's delight. They retired for the night more exhausted than usual after all the fun.

The next morning's walk was along flat sandy riverside and as we tramped along I listened to Tom describing to Sudsy the snowboard he was hoping to get for his birthday, just a week away. We reached the Flying Fox and found the river snaking peacefully with barely a white horse in sight, but opted to use the cable bridge anyway. Although the Baltis slipping off their shoes and wading across lower down made it look like a pleasant paddle, I was sure it was painfully cold and rocky underfoot. 'Providing David gets across in the box in one piece I will assume it is safe,' I shouted up ahead to Ashraf. He gave me a grimace as David climbed aboard. Kate's verdict after she shot across in the box with her minder Ibrahim was 'Brilliant'. It was then Tom's and my turn and I had to agree with my daughter.

From here we all trooped in a line along the rocky paths that led towards the Biafo glacier. The route seemed longer than we had remembered and, as it was an incredibly hot, sticky day, we were all down to shorts and T-shirts. We ploughed on, stopping once more near the Korophon army post for lunch, the spot where we believed Tom had picked up the bug that led to his sickness. Despite the almost suffocating humidity we ordered him and Kate not to go anywhere near the water. They grumbled at this but recognized the stern tone in our voices.

Our next hurdle was the glacier, a huge morass of rocks and ice. My worry was that the heat would melt the ice and make the surface even more unstable. As I suspected, it was very unpleasant. Everything was loose and slippery and we had to pick our way with consummate care. One moment my boots would stand on what looked like firm rocks, only to feel them slip and slide beneath me. This time the ugly grey scree-filled expanse was desolate; we really were at the very tail-end of the trekking season. It was a relief to get back on firm ground and out of the burning sun and from there the path dropped steeply and we found ourselves in a narrow, well-shaded gorge. We slung off our rucksacks and opened up our drinks bottles for some much-needed rehydration while Tom and Kate scrambled up the humbug-striped rocks. That night we would be staying at the camp site known locally as 'The Fort' at 3050 metres (10 000 feet), although neither a garrison nor a castle had ever existed here. Legend has it that it was the home of the King of the Fairies and the gorge we were walking through had been cut by his sword to create a way for his minions to pass through the mountains. It certainly was incredible that in this almost impassable range there should be such a cleanly sliced natural pathway.

Cally, who was clearly torn between letting me and the team or her sister down, now decided to head off in an attempt to make it back for the wedding. We said our hurried farewells and, taking Ashraf's chosen porter with her, she set off at speed and disappeared over the ridge in the direction of Askoli and Tongol. The rest of us continued more slowly, knowing camp was less than an hour away. The paraffin lamp would not work for dinner so we had to break out some aromatic hand-crafted candles that Suds had bought in Scotland as a means of keeping midges at bay when camping.

The dear old goat, which we thought was a 'Judas' to encourage the two sheep to follow us, sadly met its end here. It was quickly dispatched for the porters' end-of-trek celebration dinner – however, he must have put up a good fight because the ersatz slaughterman managed to get his thumb in between the goat's throat and his pretty sharp knife. He staggered across to the mess tent holding out a bloody hand and it looked as if he had almost severed his thumb. David and Cath swung into action but by the time they had staunched the flow the cut was found to be no more than a glorified tear. We never saw the goat again but the porter, who seemed enormously proud of his snow-white bandaged thumb, would wiggle it every time he saw us. After our candlelit dinner Ashraf entertained us by explaining the local treatment for cuts. In the Baltoro, he said, the locals wrapped the wound in cotton and set it alight, while in his home area of Hunza they covered them with goat's shit and in fishing areas around Karachi they used diesel...

The next morning I lay in bed, drinking in the view of the magnificent peaks framed by the tent door, while behind me Kate was already awake and chattering on about ballet again. 'Why do some people just go on tiptoes and others go on really high top-tiptoes, Dad?' she asked, flicking through the pictures in her library book on ballet, which I discovered was the prompt for her sudden interest. Another poser I felt ill-equipped to deal with so early in the day...The weather was slightly overcast as we laced up our walking boots and I felt a moment's sadness at the thought that this would be our last day on foot, for we would soon be saying farewell to the Baltoro. The barren rocks gradually gave way to a softer, lusher landscape with the bushes turning the full spectrum of rich autumnal colours. Underneath a big granite overhang we had to sidestep a herd of yaks, looking very much like small American buffalo, before venturing onto our final major obstacle, the high rock buttress. We wound our way up the path for a high traverse through the cliffs and Tom, sensing the dangers were nearly over, decided to play the little rascal and skip off along the matchstick-thin path ahead of us, even ignoring the terrifyingly sheer drop to one side. Only a sharp word from Suds and I persuaded him to come back and walk between our protective cordon, but he continued to tease and bait us with his daredevil exploits. I could not relax until we were back down on the sandy desert floor before our final ascent up the grassy banks to Askoli.

Just outside the village the porters all stopped by a rushing stream and washed their hands and faces, brushed their hair and replaited their pigtails before slinging on their pack frames and heading towards the beckoning 'speakeasies'. The decaying decadence of this filthy village had not found a place in my affections and was unlike anywhere else we had passed through. Everything about it had an air of neglect and most of it was falling to rack and ruin. Even the old grain mills we had seen on our arrival were left unattended and unrepaired.

Once again I had to fulfil local protocol and visit the mayor before we could push on to our camp at Tongol. David and Cath dug their heels in and refused to attend, explaining they were so disgusted at the state he kept the village it would be hypocritical of them as doctors to take tea with him. Ashraf shrugged his shoulders and pointed them up and round the corner to the camping area where he told them some of his porters would make them something to drink. As a guest of the Pakistani Government I felt I would have to respect the honour of being invited to visit this local headman whose family had been the hereditary rulers for centuries. He welcomed me back to his mayoral balcony with his gloved handshake and soft creaking voice.

As I was led yet again to the garden seat in the corner, I noticed all the village children had climbed up the ladders on the outside walls to watch us. With Ashraf acting as interpreter I asked, 'Why are the children not at school?' The mayor gave me a watery smile and launched into a long explanation. It turned out that a wealthy Dutch climber had given the village five thousand US dollars to build a school, so the mayor and his advisors had planned an ambitious two-roomed facility, complete with upper floors and balconies. However, they had not worked out the actual building costs beforehand and the money had run out before they reached the top of the windows. 'Where are the children getting their lessons now?' I asked, incredulous at the lack of forward planning. 'Outside,' came the mayor's matter-of-fact reply. He started to get tetchy when I asked

him how long the school day lasted, and when he told me one hour –
so that they could spend the rest of the day working in his fields – I
could see why.

Suddenly switching the conversation to more encouraging
matters, he explained he was building a camp site for the village that
would help bring in much-needed cash and offered to show it to me.
We walked up the slight hill at the back of the village and passed a
wall with the cemented skulls and horns of the rare Ibex sheep on the
gates. Through these was a scruffy terraced camping area and beside
it, a long thin building with a veranda. The mayor proudly showed
me this toilet block, which had five or six sitting stalls on the outside
for people to wash in, one squat toilet and a hole for a shower. Even
these facilities were only half-finished and the rest of the place was
covered in deep puddles because there was no drainage. I explained
as kindly as I could that this did not seem to match up to the
expectations and standards of most modern expeditions. My
comments were too much for the mayor, who turned his back on me
with a dismissive wave of his hand and drifted off into the crowd
looking like a child who has had his favourite lollipop taken from him.

I looked around for David and Cath, who should have been there,
and discovered them swamped by local people pressing them for
medical treatment. They were doing their best until one flash guy in
a nylon tracksuit and sunglasses pushed his way to the front with a
small baby in his hands. 'He has banged his head. We need some
medicine to make him well,' he demanded. Even I could see that the
child had been severely brain-damaged from birth. The little mite
was a heart-wrenching sight, his body a sickly grey colour as it hung
like a rag doll in his father's arms. David and Cath looked despairing
and wondered how the man could lie about the baby's condition. They
knew there was nothing they could do for the child but the people
seemed to think our two doctors could produce a Western drug that
would make everything all right as easily as a magician could produce
a rabbit out of a hat. 'Ashraf, get our belongings, it's time to get out of
this place,' I shouted. I asked him to tell the local people that, if they

needed to see a doctor, David and Cath would be at Tongol later that afternoon. Without losing any of his cool he gathered up his porters and soon we were off.

On either side of the track the leaves were turning lovely autumn shades, in particular a startlingly bright lemon-yellow. It looked like Vermont in the autumn and the beauty came as a welcome contrast to the harsh abrasive village we had just left. I walked quickly to put as much distance between Askoli and ourselves as possible. David and Cath were given an enthusiastic wave by one family working in the fields who wore smiles from ear to ear. It was only when Cath looked more closely that she realized she had treated one of the girls with a course of antibiotics on our way in for a severe face rash and it had now virtually disappeared.

Our route back to Tongol brought us along a path high above the village and, as we started our descent, we spotted a familiar dark-blue tent pitched on our site far below. It had to be Cally. When we reached it the door was open and, sure enough, lying inside were Cally's belongings, but there was no sign of their owner. We set up camp and she reappeared half an hour later, having had afternoon tea at the police post. She had arrived in Tongol the night before, only to be told the jeep road had collapsed near Hoto and no vehicles were able to get through. 'Oh well, at least I tried,' was her resigned comment.

The dinner gong went so we all trooped into the mess tent for the usual pasta and tomatoes or chicken and chips. Just as we were about to tuck in, a dark silhouette appeared outside and coughed lightly. I ventured out to find the local policeman standing there. 'Ah, Mr James, I have one of the jeep drivers here. He has managed to get within three hours walk of Tongol and says he can take Miss Cally out if she wants to go now with some of the porters.' I called Cally and told her of the development. Within minutes she was packed and ready to go, setting off into the darkness with a coterie of paid-off porters also heading to Skardu. I was not to see her again until we arrived back in Scotland. What follows describes her journey from when she left us after the Biafo glacier.

'As I set off with my porter I glanced back at the scene – porters carrying half their body weight, yaks grazing peacefully and the stunning mountain backdrop. I was very sad to leave but I had told my only sister Kirsten that if there was any way I could make it to her wedding I would. She had planned a large traditional Scottish wedding and was getting married in Dunblane Cathedral, followed by an evening ceilidh for over 250 people. It was to be a gathering of the clans as she was the first of our generation of extended family to get married. Now that we were on our return journey, the thought nagged me that I should at least try and get back, although I knew travelling in Pakistan could be far from straightforward.

'I walked quickly with my porter but we were soon joined by two hunters with shotguns slung over their backs who said they were keen to practise their English. They offered me some bread and orange squash but I heeded Dave and Cath's warning and decided to stick to the water from the mountain streams. In Askoli the women were at work as usual while the men sat on their steps discussing 'world problems'. When I arrived in Tongol there was no-one at the camp site apart from the local policeman and his two friends, who were playing a board game. I immediately had three volunteers to help me put up my tent and was told there should be a jeep the next day, although a Pakistani had been waiting three days for one. I settled down for the evening and started reading Alison's book, *A Hard Day's Summer*, but was interrupted when the policeman's servant came round and offered me green tea. A short while later I had just finished my dinner, compromising a chocolate bar and a muesli bar, when the servant returned and said I had been invited to dinner. I thought it would be rude to refuse so I walked over to the tent where the policeman was sitting cross-legged with his friends. The meal was served: rice, bread and then the meat – a goat's head, complete with eyes, tongue, horns and hair. At that moment I wished I was a vegetarian and, after eating my rice, tried to indicate that I was full, eventually only managing a few mouthfuls of the tongue. The others seemed surprised at my reluctance to dig in but the head did not go to waste. Every last morsel was consumed, finishing off with the horns, which were broken and picked out rather as one might eat a lobster.

'The policeman had been living in his simple bamboo-frame tent for over six months, signing the trekkers in and out and, after more green tea, he showed me the book. It contained the names of over 800 trekkers and he pointed out Alison's name among them. Like everyone else he had been greatly saddened by her death. I woke to tea next morning and a crowd of curious locals who had come to see this lone woman staying in their midst. The day wore on. The policeman played Ludo with his friends and I was kept topped up with sweet tea but there was no sign of a jeep. Eventually it came to light that there had been a landslide and the road was closed, an apparently normal event. The advance porters for the rest of the team arrived to set up camp and Jim's party joined me soon after. I felt any chances of getting to my sister's wedding were thwarted. Ashraf suggested that I draft a telegram for her, as he was sending out a runner. 'Have a great day, tried to get there, stopped by landslide, see you soon, Cally,' was all I could say. At that point I felt it was fate and obviously not meant to be. I settled back to life in the camp. Then, a change of plan: the jeep driver had arrived, complete with flip-flops, shalwar qamis and briefcase. He was going to walk back to his jeep with five other porters and the Pakistani who had been waiting. Ashraf said that if I wanted to go, this would be my last chance. It was 5.00 p.m. and getting dark and there was a three-hour walk to the jeep, but it was another chance and I knew I had to try. I threw my things together, said my goodbyes and raced off after the porters.

'They were a nice chatty bunch and one started up a conversation in very broken English. We headed off the main track and down a narrow goat-path that involved climbing a steep slope, which the driver found difficult with his flip-flops and briefcase. This was a short cut and sadly we must have bypassed Alison's plaque, which I had hoped to see. As we walked on it began to spit with rain and I was worried the less-than-stable hillside would start to slip. I asked my friendly porter how long we would be. 'Only ten minutes,' he replied. An hour later we were still walking and, when I asked him again, I got the same response. This, I realized, was the equivalent of, 'It's just around the corner'. By this time it was getting very dark and I picked my way carefully along the side of the gorge. All of a sudden, the porters started to run and shouted at me to do the same. There was a thunder of stones behind me. It was a landslide but, luckily, confined to just a few large, loose stones. Ahead in the darkness was a light streak stretching down the hillside and into the river. I asked if this was the landslide. It was. To me it looked totally unstable. What am I doing here? I wondered. Did my sister really want me to arrive at her wedding in a box?

'At this point I thought seriously about turning back, but decided I had come this far and could only push on. We tackled the landslide by running across it, one at a time. It felt like trying to ski on an avalanche-prone slope but we all got to the other side safely. I breathed a sigh of relief but there was still no jeep. I asked where it was. 'Just ten minutes,' came the inevitable answer. We came across a huge boulder field and the porter volunteered, 'another landslide'. At this point I decided to dig out my head torch. Big mistake. I was pushed to the front to lead the way. It was like being in a mine shaft – there was thick dust everywhere and I could only see a few feet in front, my lamp picking out rubble the size of a garden shed. Finally, at the other side, a welcome sight: the jeep. I was given the honour of the front seat and the porters piled into the back. The journey was as hair-raising as I had remembered but I had no choice but to put all my faith in the flip-flopped driver, although every so often the vehicle would be unable to manage a steep bend and the porters had to jump out and manhandle it into place.

'Around 11.00 p.m. we arrived in a largish village that I assumed was Shigar and offloaded a few more passengers. It was also time for a tea stop and I followed the driver to a dilapidated-looking hotel. The porters forced open the door where I noticed five or six Pakistanis on the floor trying to sleep. The hotel manager arrived with some tea and dry sponge cake. It seemed a strange situation, all huddled together in the relative squalor while a few Pakistanis snored at our feet, but I felt quite comfortable all the same. At half-past midnight we rolled up at the K2 Motel and honked the horn. The gates were opened by the duty manager and I was led to my room – Ashraf's grapevine must have warned them I was coming. The next day arrived all too early; I had requested an alarm call at 6.30 a.m. to catch the 9.00 a.m. flight to Islamabad. I was driven to the airport where I was met by one of Ashraf's men, only to learn that the 737 was full. After all that! Fortunately, a few words from my new-found guardian secured me a place. I learned later one of his friends had given up his seat for me and I was incredibly grateful for his kind gesture.

'Arriving in hot and sticky Islamabad was such a contrast to cool, clear Skardu. I asked about flights and learned there was one to Manchester the following day, Thursday. The only money I had was Scottish bank notes so I had to resort to my credit card for a night's stay in the city, booking in to the Paradise Hotel which had been recommended by my taxi driver. As it was near the local bazaar I popped in to buy a few last presents and, despite the curiosity factor of my blonde hair, was left completely unhassled. The eleven-hour flight to Manchester arrived at 5.00 p.m. the following day and I took a shuttle to Edinburgh that got me there just in time for my sister's hen night and all the plans she had in store for me – cake decorating, table-laying and entertaining. I didn't have time to feel jet-lagged whether I wanted to or not.'

Back at Tongol the rest of our party was saying goodbye to the porters, who were being paid off. They came and shook hands before making the journey to their villages for the winter. We were left with only Ashraf's core team of the Hushe boys, who set about arranging facilities for us to have a big wash as two weeks had passed without Tom, Kate or I having a bath. Ashraf stoked all the camp stoves into life and huge billy cans of water were placed on them to warm. Meanwhile, Ibrahim set up our 'Agincourt' tent over one of the ditches in the middle of a field. The hot water was taken in the cans and left with a large plastic jug so we could pour it over ourselves. I led Tom and Kate along to the novel contraption, got them undressed and placed their clothing on a chair outside so they could wash themselves in the jugs of water. I dried and dressed them, then it was my turn. It felt delicious, especially as I was able to unpack a clean set of clothing and put that on as well. The whole operation had taken most of the morning so we had an easy afternoon around camp – all of us except David and Cath, whose medical expertise was once again required. Tongol's headman, who, incidentally, owned all the land we were camping on, had been out pruning apple trees with his grandson when the youngster slipped off the branch and fell down the trunk, impaling the inside flesh of his right forearm on a sharp pruned stump. He was taken home to his mother in shock and she treated it with the traditional burning cotton, which, until now, we assumed Ashraf had exaggerated. By the time David and Cath saw the wound it had become severely infected and the remains of the charred cloth had to be removed before they could treat the wound. But when David produced a needle to give the boy a local anaesthetic he shrunk away in fear, never having seen one before. After some choice words from Ashraf he agreed reluctantly to the treatment. They cleaned the wound and Cath put in stitches but the problem then was how these could be removed after we had gone. Our doctors solved the problem in a ingenious way by inserting stitches into an apple and teaching the local policeman how to take them out.

The local children remained fascinated with Tom and Kate and the longer we stayed, the more confident they became. The interest was mutual and I could see curiosity drawing Tom and Kate towards these gathered youngsters. I left my offspring to their own devices and by the time the dinner gong went they were relaxed and conversing with their new friends through smiles and basic hand signs.

The following day Ashraf's remarkable information grapevine was able to tell us that the BBC boys had successfully filmed K2 and should be back at camp by 11.00 o'clock the next morning. This meant we had one more day at Tongol before we set off down the now-repaired (we hoped) jeep road for Skardu. The plaque Benazir Bhutto had ordered for Alison had been erected a few hours' walk away near Hoto, so I decided to make a quiet visit there with Tom and Kate before we made our formal one with the television cameras on us. However, as we set off, any hopes of making this a private occasion were dashed when we noticed half the village following us down rough gravel road. I could only feel honoured that they took such an interest. It was hot and the walk farther than we thought but we took it steady and slow. We circled around a couple of magnificent rock buttresses before coming to the cliffside at the edge of the jeep road where the plaque was. It had been carefully placed so that every jeep passenger or trekker along this route would see its simple but moving message:

Mother of Mountains
Such wonders you conceive
How can one so small
Dream of measuring their scale?

In fond memory of
Alison Hargreaves
Who died on her way down after successfully scaling
the summit of Chogori – Mount Godwin Austin – K2 on
August 13 1995.

I found it incredibly touching that the young, talented girl I remembered from all those years ago who set out to climb mountains and who died in Pakistan should have a plaque dedicated to her from the people of this country. I explained to Tom and Kate what it stood for and they drew their own little messages in the sand beneath it. We stood for a few moments, my climber's eyes wandering over the rock and, just as I was about to turn to leave, I noticed a distinctive hand-jamming crack running up the side of the rock next to it. This was the style of climbing Alison liked more than any other so I knew she would have approved of the location.

We made our way slowly back to the village with our entourage of curious onlookers still in tow. Tom and Kate were tired so I put them to bed early and enjoyed my last evening in the remote Baltoro valley. It was a clear, still night and Orion was once again above my head.

CHAPTER FIFTEEN

ON THE ROAD AGAIN

We shall not cease from exploration
And the end of all our exploring
Will be to arrive where we started
And know the place for the first time.

T.S. ELIOT

I never managed to fathom out how Ashraf's grapevine worked but his information was spot-on. At almost 11.00 a.m. exactly the BBC team appeared on the ridge shepherded by their Hushe porters, who were keeping up a cracking pace. El Tel looked wild-eyed — he had been breaking trail from the front and had turned a deep walnut-brown, despite attempts to keep the sun off with his Lawrence of Arabia headgear. Chris Openshaw was limping behind him, having gashed his toe, Adrian 'Ding Dong' Bell had torn some ligaments and sported a dirty bandage around his knee while the 'Boy' Andy had grown an excuse for a beard but was grinning as usual.

We were packed and ready to go except for a table and chairs, some food and a few Thermos flasks of hot tea for the BBC crew. Ashraf had wanted to leave the mess tent and set the table for them but I said it would do them good to 'suffer' a little. They dropped their stuff and quickly downed the much-needed refreshment as their equipment was packed into the luggage jeep. Meanwhile, the rest of us felt it was time to show our appreciation for the Hushe boys' efforts during the trek and asked Ashraf to call Ibrahim, Little Ibrahim and Abdul over. We had put together some gifts from the spare mountaineering clothing we were carrying and asked Tom and Kate to present them. Our two cook boys, Little Ibrahim and Abdul, were clearly chuffed with their fleece sweaters still in their designer-labelled plastic wrappings and we did not see Ibrahim without his new Sprayway Gortex jacket again.

Cath, David, Tom, Kate and I piled into one jeep, Ashraf, Sudsy and the rest of the Hushe boys packed into the baggage truck and the BBC boys in a larger pick-up followed up the rear. Then the local policeman appeared bearing a farewell gift. It was a set of huge Ibex horns, great big curls that must have been over 6 feet across. The rest of the team could not hide their smirk, knowing I was a vegetarian and vehemently against blood sports. 'Thank you very much, I will find an honoured place for them,' I told him, not specifying where, and they too were mounted on the luggage vehicle. I took one last look around and said a lingering farewell to our home for the past few days.

Our jeeps rattled onto the rough gravel road and across the white flat sulphur bed below the hot springs before we climbed once more into the mountains. Alison would be chuckling away to herself if she saw this pantomime, I thought as we bounced along. The weather was overcast and the high peaks were hidden as we stepped out of our jeeps to see Alison's plaque for the second time, now with the cameras on us. Kate clutched the last of her mother's silk flowers, a yellow one, and placed it in the little crack I had noticed, filling it in with stones so it would remain hidden. Tom and Kate were pleased to see their little sand drawings had not been touched. It was very odd to think that the passengers of every jeep going up or down this road would see the plaque and be reminded of Alison and her achievements. For the final time we turned and left.

From here the jeep road climbed steeply. Most of the last third of our inward journey had been in darkness so I was eager to see what the route looked like in daytime, although as we started to make our precarious way along the narrow ledges I wondered if that was altogether wise. The landscape around us was savage in the extreme, with huge drops, dangerous-looking overhangs and loose scree. Our jeep drivers were clearly still worried about the state the road was in. At this point it was incredibly bumpy and the corrugated effect caused by the ruts seemed worse than I had remembered. However, my main concern was the width of the track, which looked no wider than a footpath and seemed to be fraying at the edges right before our eyes. We climbed higher and looked down on the huge boulders that littered the swirling river. Each time a jeep drove along here the wheels would slough a bit more off the bank, forcing the drivers to cut into the hillside just to keep the vehicle from falling more than 300 feet. This erosion meant that, instead of being flat, the road was now tilting towards the water far below. The sight eventually became too much for David. He suddenly leapt up from his bench seat behind the driver and moved over to the side hugging the wall, sending the driver into confusion and panic as this redistribution of 18 stones sent the car veering wildly. We held our breath as the driver struggled to stay on track and there was an almost collective sigh of relief once he was back in control. From behind the wheel came the muttering of what sounded like prayers and there were certainly a few 'Inshallahs'. We all turned and looked at David. 'I felt the vehicle would be better balanced on this side, nothing to do with the fact I was sitting directly above a massive drop,' he assured us with a shy grin.

The vehicles now had to inch down a steep embankment and on to a flat stage, which should have meant smoother driving – except that the track had almost completely disappeared under a rock fall. The drivers had to pick their way carefully through the boulders rather like a slalom and to us in the back it felt as though we were being dragged across a cheese grater. Another climb to a big spur and we were on the narrow winding section of track where Suds, Tom and I had got out and walked on the way in. Once again we had to negotiate the extremely tight hairpin bends by each vehicle accelerating then reversing in their battle to get round. Suddenly, we saw the BBC pick-up, which had taken the lead after we stopped at the plaque to Alison, lurch and stall. One of the wheels was hanging over the precipice. Very carefully, the boys shifted along and climbed out of the inside door, one by one. Even Chris Terrill's walnut-brown tan seemed to have paled. 'I think the gods are looking down on us this morning,' he managed. Looking over the edge he added quietly into his fleece, 'Thank you, Alison'. The steering had gone and the pick-up was only prevented from going over the edge by a few strategically placed boulders. We certainly seemed to have been blessed on this trip.

The non-English speaking driver had a poke around under his vehicle then, pulling himself out, explained as best he could that the steering rod had fractured. Fishing under the driver's seat he pulled out a metal coat hanger, a rusty adjustable spanner and a pair of pliers that looked as though they had come out of a Christmas cracker. Suds found some 5-millimetre climbing line and handed this to him. He shuffled back under the chassis and fiddled away. 'It looks great, the coat hanger is doing sterling service, I have got every confidence,' I shouted to the BBC boys after inspecting his handiwork, relieved I was not travelling in that particular jeep. Surprisingly, despite my assurances, the lads were not convinced. 'Do you want to swap jeeps?' they asked hopefully.

'No, no, no,' I bluffed hastily. 'I need to stay with the rest of the team to give them moral support.' Refusing to get back on board until the makeshift repairs had proved their worth, they scrambled up the road on foot as their driver tested out the pick-up on the next few bends. The coat hanger and climbing line seemed to hold so they reluctantly clambered back on board, although I noticed they were less boisterous for the rest of the drive and Chris Terrill no longer did his Lawrence of Arabia impression standing gesticulating from the back.

We drove on past people in brightly coloured shalwar qamis working in the terraced fields – it looked as though it had been a good harvest. Bushes of lavender reappeared along the roadside and I plucked the flowers as we drove by, rubbing their mauve heads between my palms to release the scent. I had done it many times in Provence during my regular visits there but the aroma was never quite as fresh as it was now. Tom had a quick yawn, unimpressed by the landscape. I think it was a case of, 'been there, done that, got the video', so to speak. We thudded onto the first of the wooden suspension bridges, wobbled as the cables took the strain and the planks creaked, then accelerated up onto the other bank. A large yak stood grazing in a field across the river as we passed a village built under a lone boulder standing at least 100 feet high. 'Look Dad, he's got horns nearly as big as yours,' piped up Kate, referring to the Ibex antlers dominating the baggage truck. 'Perhaps I could lend him them,' I responded, as the image of having to carry the monstrosities through Heathrow airport leapt into my mind.

Saleem, Ashraf's assistant, had invited us to his house in Dasso for tea, so we squeezed the jeeps into the narrow main street and were led into the dark recesses of one of the squat, square houses. I sunk cross-legged into piles of oval bolsters that massaged my painfully bumped and bruised backside. The room was decorated lavishly in deep-red wall coverings punctuated by Islamic scriptures, while on the floor were thick-pile, richly patterned carpets. Tea was poured; I took a sip and found it refreshingly minty. Then a tray of tiny apples and pears was brought in. I could smell their fragrance as they were carried across the room and as soon as I took a mouthful I realized why the area had such a reputation for delicious fruit. Cath was invited to visit the women in the house, which I could see pleased her, and she was taken off to the private rooms. Once again I was overwhelmed by the hospitality of these people.

As we crossed a dilapidated bridge on our way out of Dasso one of the planks beneath us popped out of place and our rear wheel fell through the space, sending the chassis dropping with considerable force and causing all of us to jump in terror. We pulled ourselves together and the jeep out of its rut and continued down the Shigar valley where the Haramosh range came into view once more. Dusk was falling and soon we could see only what our watery headlights picked out.

It felt like hours before we crossed the desert valley again and could pick up speed. The rich aroma I had been unable to identify on our journey in, which Ashraf now informed me was sage, assaulted our nostrils. Sheep pens beside the road were full of beasts and the odd dim light could be seen behind the doors of the dry-stone dwellings beside them. Clearly everyone was tucked up for the night. Eventually two or three vehicles passed us and the road began to feel more solid under the tyres so we knew Skardu must be approaching.

Sure enough, a short while later we were rattling into the courtyard of the K2 Motel. I jumped out to be told Cally had managed to get a flight out and was on her way home, which cheered us all. Ice-cold cans of non-alcoholic beers were ordered and as Ashraf, Sudsy and the BBC boys drove up they were snatched thirstily and glugged down. After hot showers all round and a convivial meal I relaxed; we were back in civilization and everyone was still in one piece. Our adventure was over, or so I thought.

The following day was to be spent resting and I was doing just that on the terrace when our favourite duo, the slim, smartly dressed deputy commissioner and the rotund chief of police, turned up to see how our trek had gone. 'Mr Ballard, how nice to see you again, I trust everything went well,' roared the police chief, a white grin splitting his black beard. They led me through to the dining room where we were joined by David and Cath as a table was set for us in the corner. Through the large bay windows I could still see the fabulous view over the Indus to the Haramosh mountains that I had been lapping up from my pew on the terrace. Over tea we told our two official friends how the trek had gone and they seemed pleased, although the deputy commissioner's face furrowed when I described the conditions we had found at Askoli and our disappointment in the place. A few more sweet pastries were popped into their mouths, chewed and swallowed, then they were off, bidding us farewell and a safe journey.

The following morning I was woken by Tom tugging at my bedclothes. Usually the most reluctant of the three of us to get out of bed, he was flushed and excited as today was his birthday. We were due to leave for the airport for our flight back to Islamabad but one look out of the window and I knew we were grounded. The sky was overcast and, while perfectly acceptable anywhere else, it would prove impossible to fly because of the local ban on the use of radar. We all gathered in the dining room for breakfast and discussed the options over our eggs and cornflakes – apart from Tom, who was tucking into a pile of sweets left at his place by the management after learning it was his birthday. A grinning Ashraf strode in bearing more gifts for Tom: a polo stick and ball and the traditional local gift of a necklace studded with rupee notes.

Ashraf advised us that it would be wise to consider travelling by road as the forecast for the next few days was not good. Chris Terrill, beginning to worry about time, also thought this would be a good option so we agreed we would set off for Gilgit at 11.00 a.m. where Ashraf assured us we could catch a minibus to take us down the Karakoram highway to Islamabad and Rawalpindi. Some American Embassy officials and an Italian trekker also decided to do the same and their jeep headed up the dirt road ahead of us. I found it incredibly sad driving past the bazaar, the polo field and the terraced fields of Skardu, wondering how long it would be before I saw the place again. I had already vowed I would return with Tom and Kate for further adventures.

We followed the Indus along the flood plains until the flat white sand narrowed and the river cut into the chocolate-brown rock. It looked like toothpaste being squeezed out of a tube. I had one last look back before the track wound after it into the gorge. As we rounded the bend we noticed the front jeep had been pulled up at a police checkpoint ahead. The sentry was demanding passports and identification. I climbed out and tried to look impressive, explaining who I was, and immediately the tone changed. I was simply asked to sign their sheet and we were ushered through. We were leaving the valley, so this would be the last time I could get away with doing my 'Grand Fromage' impression. From now on we were just ordinary travellers like anyone else, except, of course, that we were still able to rely on the experience and guile of Ashraf. The ride was an astonishing journey through centuries of life as we followed the Indus through the rocky divide. Faint tracks, carvings and ancient settlements could all be spotted across the river, giving us a little taste of why the Indus was called the 'Cradle of Civilization'.

A couple of hours later the jeeps pulled up beside a little stone shack for lunch. It was clearly a café of some kind as we could smell baking and a pile of pots was stacked up underneath a waterfall crashing from the rocks above. Wooden chairs lined the road and we had just sat down on them to unpack our lunch boxes when Ashraf came over. 'Mr Jim, would you like some nan and dahl?' he enquired, polite as ever. The smell of baking had reached our nostrils and, like me, everyone wanted to taste the bread – although we decided we had had enough of dahl. 'Oh, I think you should try some,' Ashraf pressed, so we took his advice and soon steaming aluminium dishes of golden chickpea dahl were laid next to the hot nans. It was magnificent and we polished off bowls and bowls, even using our sandwiches to mop it up once the nan had been finished. We were to learn later that the café was known throughout Baltistan for its excellent cooking. The little stone shack was filled with a beehive-shaped tandoori oven and a big hob heated by a paraffin stove. It was so small the kitchen workers had to sit on top of the covered clay oven as they kneaded the dough into shape. Our mini tour over, Ashraf was keen to hurry us back to our jeeps for we had a long journey ahead of us.

It was nearly 7.00 p.m. and just getting dark by the time the first lights of Gilgit flickered at the top of the valley. Sure enough, a minibus was waiting for us, along with a couple of Ashraf's cronies – once again his mysterious grapevine had worked. We climbed on board the bus, Suds, Kate and I in the two back seats, Cath and Tom on the one in front, with David in front of them, while the BBC boys managed to fill up the rest. As we drove out on to the tarmac of the Karakoram highway the skies opened in a torrent, complete with flashes of lightning and rumbling thunder. Ashraf ordered the driver to stop at the now-closing bazaar, jumped out and disappeared into the rain, only to reappear a couple of minutes later laden down with soggy bags of apples and pears for the journey. 'I have a friend here,' he informed us, shaking the water from his spiky hair and broad shoulders. We asked no more questions but appreciated the fruit. Unperturbed by the storm outside, Tom and Kate curled up on their seats and went to sleep.

The hotel Ashraf had planned to take us to for supper was closed when we drew up four hours later so, with his usual style, he set about waking up the owner to serve us. Thinking this was a bit extreme, I pointed out that a wayside café would do us fine as long as the food was as good as the meal we had on the Indus road earlier. Ashraf looked horrified but when we all explained that we had really enjoyed our lunch he shrugged his shoulders and we clambered back on board as he directed the driver to a little brightly lit timber shack.

We were just tucking into our nan and dahl when the beam of headlights shone straight into our faces and a police van pulled up to a sudden halt. Out stepped two smartly dressed armed officers who eyed us with unconcealed amazement. Ashraf stepped forward and said something that soothed their frowns and the three of them disappeared inside the café. We were only to learn later that this was the heart of bandit country; even locals avoided driving along this stretch of the highway at night and certainly no-one sat casually outside a café without an armed escort. Oops. Later, during a toilet stop, the very real dangers were brought home to us when a shop owner sidled up to Adrian Bell and asked if he wanted to buy a Kalashnikov assault rifle. Needless to say, our BBC soundman politely declined the offer and we left as soon as possible.

Sleep came but it was uncomfortable and rather fitful, not surprising considering we were trying to fit a broad-shouldered Northerner, an even broader-shouldered Scotsman and a restless Kate on two seats and an armrest. As dawn broke, so activity on the Karakoram highway picked up. The winding highway, which only opened in 1986, follows the ancient Silk Road between Pakistan and China. I was soon engrossed in the life passing outside the minibus windows as the road gradually filled up with loaded camel trains, teams of pack donkeys and herds of goats and sheep, all competing for space with the latest Western-style vehicles. Some would be travelling the full length of the highway between Rawalpindi and Kashgar in China, a distance of over 750 miles.

It was over twenty-four hours since we left Skardu and we had travelled over 440 miles and been through eleven police checks by the time we started to plough our way through the congested suburbs of Rawalpindi and pulled up at the Holiday Inn for a return to luxury living. As we collected our luggage and poured into the lobby I pressed my Ibex horns into Ashraf's hands and said, 'Please take these for your office'. He looked surprised but pleased and, as I watched him struggle away with them, my face could not hide my unconcealed relief. At last they had found an appropriate home.

CHAPTER SIXTEEN

POSSESSIONS

'Life leads the thoughtful man
on a path of many windings.'

I. CHING

I had one more difficult duty to carry out before we returned home, and that was to collect Alison's belongings. I remembered the assurance given by Abdul Quddus of Nazir Sabir Expeditions when I met him in Islamabad that they had brought them down from K2 base camp and had them at their stores. I had given Roger Courtiour a letter authorizing him to act on my behalf while we were away and he had transferred them to the British High Commission. During the trek I wondered why her totes and barrels had not been taken straight there after her death. There was little I could do but hope that nothing had been stolen or tampered with.

It was a duty I had to undertake but I felt slightly uneasy about carrying it out cold in front of the television cameras as I did not know how such personal reminders of Alison's life would affect me. It was with something less then enthusiasm that I climbed into the minibus with Ashraf and the BBC crew to make the journey across the city to collect her things on the second day after our return to Islamabad. Tom and Kate had been left with David, Suds and Cath by the High Commission club's swimming pool. After a half-hour drive, we were welcomed by a smartly dressed Pakistani security guard and ushered through high gates into the green, shady compound, and then into a nondescript modern building where we all crammed into a small office as Alison's barrels and totes were piled up before me. Her diaries and films, which had been found in her tent among her equipment at base camp, had been kept in the High Commission safe. The BBC boys insisted they filmed me as I collected them, nearly locking themselves in the strong room as the security time switches began to close the heavy lead doors before they could get themselves and their equipment out. Only the quick intervention of an official prevented them from having to spend the night there.

Any doubts I had about Abdul Quddus's integrity after our earlier meeting proved, happily, to be unfounded. Every last fleece and letter had been listed and catalogued and, as far as I could see, everything I expected to find was there. Her high-altitude sleeping bags and much of her climbing kit are unlikely ever to be recovered because they would have been at one of the camps high on the mountain and would have been collected by Alison had she made her way down.

She had taken three cameras with her but I knew her newest compact had been borrowed by an American because she had told me on the phone how she could not help laughing at his horror-struck face as he watched his own camera going 'b'doing, b'doing' (as she put it) down the mountain when he dropped it. He had left Alison's for her to collect at the Shalimar Hotel in Islamabad. Her favourite Olympus XA camera, which she had used for the last twelve years and taken the pictures on top of Everest with, would have been round her neck when she died, as would a video camera she had been using. But she had used plenty of film and luckily most of it had been left at base camp. The rolls were piled up next to the diaries in the safe alongside her video footage.

The photographs would need developing but her videos could be watched. I didn't know how I would feel viewing some of Alison's last movements on screen but settled down to concentrate and switched on the video machine. I was pleased for her because she had captured some interesting and rare shots. There she was, all wrapped up on the mountain, talking into the camera and, on another occasion, down at base camp sunbathing. There were even some close-up shots of her eating her evening meal of chicken casserole – a rare sight because she had only started eating meat again on Everest when she felt she couldn't get enough decent vegetable protein and thought she would keep it up until she came back from K2. It looked as though she had taken much of the footage on her solo attempt at the summit and there were some spectacular views from high on the Abruzzi ridge over the other 8000-metre (26 247-feet) peaks when she would have been above camp four. She was looking down on the enormous mountains that had loomed over us on our trek. It was probably one of the few times such unusual views had been captured on video and it made you realize just how impressive it must have felt to stand alone at a height like that.

We did not have long as the cameras were running, so I turned my attention to her diaries. There was the one she had been writing at the time of her death on K2. She always kept the book at base camp but continued writing on bits of paper, even when she was on the mountain, and copied or stuck them into her notebook later. Her neat, square handwriting had filled over half of the blue hardback notebook. I flicked through it briefly, read the final entry, then put it down to consume in-depth at a later date. I moved on to the smaller, white hardback. This was her Everest diary, written in May when she made her record-breaking attempt on the world's highest peak. In the short time when she was back home from Everest she had not shown anyone her loose-leaf notes and had taken them to K2 base camp where she filled them into her diary. I turned the pages, finally arriving at the date I was looking for, 13 May 1995, the day she summited.

The BBC boys were eager to hear what it said. My eyes ran down the page until I found her description of her greatest climbing achievement. I read aloud:

> ...and then I saw the summit. It was beautiful with red and yellow, vivid-coloured prayer flags frozen upside down into the bottom of the cornice leading down under the summit — an old tripod, probably abandoned by a survey team, was upside down under this too — and on the summit — the various metal artefacts/oddments people had left. It was so vivid against the snow it was incredible. I felt very emotional and I burst into

*tears. Everything welled up inside me, it was too much. I couldn't hold it
any longer, crying released it all.*

*...Then I was there. Those last few metres physically such hard work
but I was determined to be there...the radio went. I spoke to Leo Dickinson
[a distinguished adventure film-maker, who was filming her from
the North Col]. I had a message for Tom and Kate. 'I am on top of the
world and I love you dearly.' I could hear yells of joy all around.*

I looked up but tried not to catch the eyes of any of the film crew. That
had been Alison's proudest moment and her words said it all. She had
always been more openly emotional than me. Tears for her came at
times of joy, such as this had been, or frustration when things got on
top of her. I turned my attention to her bags and barrels. I knew where
everything would be; she was incredibly organized and tidy and always
packed in exactly the same way for an expedition. I turned straight to
her purse. I knew what I was looking for. There it was, her wedding
ring. Alison had always taken this off on high climbs because her
fingers would swell up slightly at altitude, making any jewellery
extremely uncomfortable. A lot of climbers tend to wear them around
their necks but Alison preferred to keep all her jewellery safe with her
belongings at base camp. I was glad to see it as I felt it was important
to keep the ring for Kate when she grew older. The gold band was
simple and plain. Alison had chosen it herself in Harrogate the year
before Tom was born. With it was some loose change and a can-
opener. That was typical of her, always practical.

As with her jewellery, Alison's ordinary clothes will be put away
in safety until Kate is of an age when she can decide what she wants
to do with them. However, there are few of them because Alison was
sponsored to wear her outdoor clothing so she wore little else, as
photographs show. I feel the more of her Alison's personal things Kate
has to remind her of her mother, the better. I don't want Tom and
Kate to have just Alison's public mountaineering image to remember
her by; I want them to understand that she was also a normal, caring
mother who loved them deeply.

I moved on to the barrels. Her Walkman had a 10,000 Maniacs tape in it and a cassette of The Cranberries was beside that, both of which I think she must have been borrowed from one of the Americans at base camp because I had not heard her listening to either before. None of the BBC crew had ever heard of 10,000 Maniacs so I teased them for being a team of old fogeys, although they were new to me as well. Her bags contained mostly climbing clothing, including the custom-made suit she had worn on Everest, although there were one or two scarves and casual items she had bought in Islamabad. There was her washbag, hairdryer and favourite Alice bands. Alison always tried to make the best of herself, even at base camp, and she would try to wash, shower and change her clothes as often as possible. When other people could barely get out of their tent because of the cold, she would still try to make the effort to wash her hair, although there would be little use for a hairdryer in the electricity-free camp. I assumed she had brought that for the social functions she was expected to attend in Islamabad. Funnily enough, Kate had asked, 'Can I have Mum's hairdryer?' before we left. It seemed an odd request but I had searched our cupboards for it; now I knew why I had been unable to find it. At least Kate would be pleased.

Alison's fresh round face always photographed well. On her day she could look very beautiful. I took some shots of her just before she did the north face of the Cima Grand three or four years ago and she looked as stunning as any model I've ever seen. She was a tight size ten and while I have described her as the same as any ordinary mother, this was not entirely true for it was hard to miss her well-developed body. Every inch of her 9½ stones was toned muscle and she worked hard to keep it that way. She would step up her training as she approached an expedition but even during rest periods she would always have a daily run of between 8 and 14 miles, mostly on rough uphill terrain. She always felt better when she regularly exercised her cardiovascular system.

I rummaged in her bag. My fingers felt something solid and I pulled it out. It was her bottle of Chanel N°5, the perfume I had introduced her to as a young girl and which she had stuck with ever since. I remember even as a boy from a prefab council estate I enjoyed the smell of Chanel N°5.

She must have started collecting artefacts from the mountain because I found an old oxygen mask, so old the rubber had perished. It was likely to have been dropped by a climber in the fifties or even earlier – I know the Americans were using such masks back in the thirties. Most of the ones near base camp have been snatched up as souvenirs, so my guess was that she found it on the hill. She clearly wanted to keep it because it was in one of her favourite waterproof sacks alongside some old rock pegs and a rusting horseshoe she had also picked up. It was time to go. Alison's belongings would be flown back to Britain alongside our own. I would unpack them properly when I had a quiet moment at home.

We returned to the High Commission to find the swimming-pool area in an uproar. Tom and Kate were causing havoc, as children can do when they sense they have been left out of something important. Sudsy looked up from his seat and gave me a grimace that suggested, 'children should be boiled in oil', while normally mild-mannered David was at the end of his tether after finding the rascals had thrown his T-shirt and towel into the pool. Cath was trying her best to control them. It was time for Dad to step in. 'Pick those out of the water and say sorry to David, then to Cath and then to Sudsy,' I shouted. They obeyed meekly, knowing full well they had overstepped the mark.

That night our old friend Changez from the Ministry of Tourism was to host a farewell dinner for us on the roof restaurant of the Holiday Inn, so we decided to take a last stroll through the city before then. We quickly learned it was 'Black Wednesday' or 'Good Wednesday', depending on who you listened to, with half the city striking over the fact that Benazir Bhutto had been in power for a year while the other half celebrated. The air was tense and the streets crowded and noisy but we felt the opposing factions shouting abuse at one another were not interested in a small Western party like ours and trusted in their child-friendly attitude to bring no harm to Tom and Kate. However, we realized how explosive the situation could become when we happened across hundreds of riot police in navy-blue uniforms and visored helmets carrying long batons and shields. It was time to head back.

Before the meal the hotel management presented Tom with a birthday cake. The British high commissioner and his wife led the party singing 'Happy Birthday to You', after which Tom and Kate blew out the seven candles and cut up the cake. As we tucked into our last Pakistani dinner on the Holiday Inn roof, the shouting, horn-tooting and general hubbub below added an air of drama to our last night in this fascinating country.

CHAPTER SEVENTEEN

A NEW START

'Do not stand at my grave and weep;
I am not there. I do not sleep.
I am a thousand winds that blow.
I am the diamond glints on snow.'

ANON

'Dad, when are we gonna be home?' Kate sat in the back seat of our car. Cally had driven down to Glasgow to pick us up after we had flown from Islamabad to London and then taken the shuttle north. She had dropped us off at Nevis Range so that we could pick up our car. 'Well, Kate, in about five or six minutes I should say,' I replied. We turned off the main road and onto our private track. The sheep were still grazing in the fields on either side but the woodland had turned from deep green to russet brown and the driveway was a carpet of fallen leaves. Stone Cottage's slate roof came into view then disappeared again as we went down a dip before we finally pulled up outside the door. 'Let's get in and light a fire, it's freezing,' I told Tom and Kate, reflecting that the damp of Scotland reached your bones far more quickly than the much lower temperatures of Baltistan where the air was drier.

I unlocked the heavy wooden door and Tom and Kate clattered into the hall, dropping their rucksacks with a thud. Everything was as we had left it; our new home for our new life. Tom and Kate disappeared upstairs and I could hear them thumping about. 'Let's not get in a mess up there, please,' I shouted. 'I spent the best part of a day cleaning it before we left.' Life was back to normal.

There was a pile of mail on the tiled hall floor. I worked my way through it quickly, noting that the family allowance book had been changed to my name. Now I had no choice but to be a single parent and I knew my life would have to alter accordingly. I had always put the children first; now that responsibility had doubled. One thing Alison and I had discussed was how we wanted to bring up our children. It was something we both felt very strongly about and the matter had been brought up even before Tom was born – not because we thought one or the other of us would disappear or die, but because we wanted to make sure we both agreed. Luckily, we did. We set out to bring up our children enjoying, understanding and accepting the wild and beautiful places on this earth. The one promise we made to each other that was totally binding was that we would always continue to do that. I had renewed that vow with Alison's spirit that warm summer's night in August, sitting on the step in front of my house looking at the mountains when I said my final goodbye. It was a promise I shall not break.

Tom and Kate have already travelled to Nepal, the United States, alpine Europe and Pakistan. Now a return visit to Baltistan with them in happier circumstances is top of my agenda. I also have every intention of being back on the ski slopes this winter with the children and to continue bouldering and climbing whenever I get the chance. When they are older it will be up Tom and Kate to decide what they want to do, but I cannot think of a better upbringing and education. Later, if they want to be a carpenter or a cook, then that will be their choice. In the meantime, I want to show them what the world has to offer. That does not mean I would push Tom or Kate into following their mother up mountains. Alison and I never encouraged them to climb, we just felt that if it was something they wanted to do then they would gravitate towards it themselves.

Whatever talents they have, be it as a bricklayer or a brain surgeon, I shall do my utmost, like any proud parent, to support them. I am lucky enough to have two lovely children and I will never pressure them in any particular direction, just give them as adventurous a life as possible. In that way Alison's spirit will always stay with them and they will always have a mother to be proud of.

When Tom saw K2 he thought it was 'massive, as big as half the world, and Everest is bigger than the whole world'. He never had any doubts about what his mother did. Even after her death he thought it was 'brilliant' that she had climbed those two.

The day after our return I thought I would give Kate time to recover from jet lag, and told her she would not be going to nursery that day. But she was adamant she was going. 'I can do what I want, nobody can tell me what to do,' she thundered.

'Who told you that?' I asked.

'Mummy,' she replied. I had a wry smile. Alison would always be present in her children. Needless to say, Kate was dropped off to see her nursery chums – I knew the stubborn force I was up against. I then drove Tom to class. As I watched him run into the little school, his rucksack – full of the work he had kept up with while we were away – on his back, I mused how his schoolmates would take his tales about the trip. I remembered when we had returned from Nepal. The school taxi driver was chatting to me a few days later and she laughed and said, 'Isn't it amazing what stories youngsters come up with these days? Do you know your son has just been spinning a story, telling me he has been to Everest. What an imagination, ha ha.' Her face dropped when I told her every word he had said had probably been true.

A DOCTOR'S PERSPECTIVE

BY CATH COLLIER

I was thrown into a confusion of emotions and loyalties when Jim asked me and my husband David to accompany him to K2 with the children. We had got to know Jim, Alison, Tom and Kate when we travelled to Everest with them in 1994 and I was still in a state of shock and grief following Alison's death.

'Do you think the children are ready for it?' was my first response to Jim. He assured me that Tom was adamant he wanted to see his mum's last mountain and that it probably didn't matter where Kate was – K2 may as well be behind Ben Nevis as far as her concept of the world was concerned.

I had to seek advice. I spoke to two eminent child psychiatrists, a child psychologist, two paediatricians, the GPs at my practice and lots of relatives. The range of opinions was vast and often extreme. Professional advice was obviously highly influenced by gut reactions; people have strong feelings about whether Alison, the mother, should have climbed at all and whether Jim was acting in the children's best interests. I was not interested in these extreme views. Maybe I just listened to the views I wanted to hear, but when I spoke to Dr Dora Black, child psychiatrist at the Traumatic Stress Clinic, London, I was encouraged. She had done much research into the counselling of bereaved children which had shown there was significant benefit, at least in the short-term, from encouraging grief through counselling early on.

It has been shown that losing a parent in childhood is often associated with emotional and behavioural problems as a child. Later in life, it has also been associated with mental health problems, like depression. I felt that this trip could be seen as an opportunity for the children to work through some of their feelings about the loss. Having me as their 'special' doctor or counsellor could help support them through the difficult emotional journey and possibly help them come to terms with and improve their understanding of their mother's death.

So, with a sense of loyalty towards Alison and Jim, I agreed to go as the children's doctor. I wasn't sure what my role would turn out to be, but decided to keep some distance initially and let the children decide what they might want from me. As far as the harsh environment was concerned, I had spent seven weeks at 5460 metres (17 913 feet) with them at Everest base camp the previous autumn and they coped well and enjoyed the outdoor life, so I didn't have too many anxieties about that aspect.

When I arrived a few days before departure at Fort William, Kate didn't recognize me but Tom remembered me from the Everest trip. He understood the trip was to see K2 but when I asked what was special about the trip he would say, 'It's the second highest mountain in the world,' without mentioning his mother or her death. Kate was more spontaneous. She was very aware of various clothes her mother had bought her and wanted to take them with her on the trip. On one occasion she had a tantrum and screamed, 'Mummy, Mummy, Mummy, come back to me Mummy.' This was the first indication to me that she knew she had lost someone very important to her.

I was alone in the kitchen with her on the day before we left for Pakistan when she explained to me that she was going to see Mum and 'give her all my love for ever, and Tom is too'. I wasn't sure where this had come from; possibly brother and sister had talked about the trip together. It was very moving. I wondered then whether either or both of them fantasized about being reunited with their mother when we got to the mountain.

We had arrived in Islamabad and were at dinner when, out of the blue, Tom sent me a message. He handed a folded paper serviette to David, telling him it was 'a message for Cath'. As soon as I saw it, I knew it was significant. On the white, mountain-shaped triangular serviette was a face, drawn near the top. At the bottom was a drawing of a vehicle and a tent. The rest of the serviette had been obliterated by scribbling. Tom explained this was Chinese writing. 'What does this mean?' I asked.

'Well, that's for you to find out,' he said. It felt clear to me that he wanted to communicate and I was flattered that he felt I could be trusted to listen to his emotions. Tom thus dictated my role.

The following day we flew to Skardu and Tom sat next to me on the plane. He knew he was likely to see K2 for the first time and I could sense he was anxious and tense. When the BBC asked the family to come to the cockpit where they could now see K2, I encouraged him to go. We squeezed in behind his father and managed to see the amazing triangular peak of K2, prominent on the horizon. Tom quickly located the mountain but didn't want to stay long, so we returned to our seats. He was quiet for a while, and then got excited as I took pictures out of the window and let him take some, which pleased him.

Once we had arrived in Skardu and were waiting in the airport lounge for our luggage, I gave the children pencils and paper and Tom immediately drew a picture of K2. This was in warm colours with a dark patch near the top. Above was a night sky, with a new moon. He seemed to get great release from this and was much more relaxed and happy and went on to draw the charismatic police chief in his blue uniform. Kate drew very abstract pictures and seemed confused as to what they could mean, but they were certainly expressive and colourful. She also seemed happier afterwards.

At the K2 Motel, with a VIP reception and the inevitable BBC film crew, the children were once again exposed to much talk about their mother and how special she was. I felt this was positive for them, although difficult. Jim often appeared to speak in a rather unemotional way and possibly the grieving that the children had been exposed to had been 'low key'. On the other hand, it was good they had a remaining parent who was very together and reliable. I was pleased I had at least made a start in helping Tom express his feelings through art.

The family were given Alison's room at the K2 Motel and this held strong significance for Tom and Kate. David sat with them as Jim popped out to collect the luggage. He thought they looked upset. Kate was curled up on the end of the bed and Tom was in a chair sucking is thumb (as per usual). David asked Kate if she was upset because this had been Mummy's room. She said yes, then asked, 'How did Mummy die?' David explained as best he knew. Then Tom piped up with, 'Mummy could still be alive up there?' As David told him how unlikely that was Tom said, 'She could have built a snow cave'. David said she would not have survived and must be dead. Then there was a silence, but not a bad one.

Later the children came up to our room and demanded the pencils and paper. Both Tom and Kate drew K2. Kate said they were drawing them to give to Mummy at base camp. David wept; Kate seemed surprised but Tom said, 'Even Daddy cries sometimes'. Kate's drawings now were very black and abstract, but Tom, having drawn K2 again, went happily into drawing the aeroplanes and helicopters that he had seen earlier.

There were times when the pressure of having a camera pointed at the family trod on the children's sensitivities. For example, on one occasion the BBC filmed a session with Jim and the children. Jim wore his usual matter-of-fact front and initially I found this apparent insensitivity upsetting. He picked up one of Tom's pictures of K2, saying that this was the one he was to leave for his mum. He happened to have picked the correct one, but he hadn't asked Tom and didn't ask Kate if she had any drawings to leave. However, he was talking about Alison to the children, which must be seen positively and it was preparing them for the climax of the trip.

Kate insisted on sitting in my lap for the ten-hour journey to Askoli and, like most four-year-olds, delighted in the fact she was depriving another – David – of my company. She spent much of the journey admiring herself in the door mirror and was oblivious to the dangers of the loose, treacherous jeep road, which threatened to disappear from under us at any time. I managed to do some opportunistic counselling at various points along the way. On the first part of the journey I encouraged her to talk about her mother. She said she was going to draw a picture of K2 with all her friends at the bottom. This she would leave at the bottom of K2 to show her mum she was not alone. She spoke of her grandma and grandpa and agreed that they loved her and Tom very much. This was a useful conversation as it reinforced to her how much support she had around her.

Later in the journey we were chatting about different types of fish and Kate mentioned sharks. She said she had seen a film about sharks where a man had his legs bitten off and then died. I asked her what it meant to die. She faltered at this, but eventually said: 'It's when you're not alive, like Mum'. I explained that, when dead, you did not feel pain. Kate said the man bitten by the shark would have felt pain when he was bitten, but that when he was dead he would feel no pain. Excellent logic from a four-year-old.

She asked if we were all going to K2 to die, like Mum did. 'No, we were going to return home at the end of the trip,' I explained. If we died, we would not be able to go home. Her mother could not go home because she was dead, I added; she had to stay on the mountain for ever. Kate seemed to accept this, quietly sucked her thumb for a while, then went off happily into an imaginary world in the mirror again.

We arrived at our first camp site in the dark and as Jim, David and Suds sorted out the luggage, Cally and I took Tom and Kate to the mess tent. Both were tired and irritable. All the talk of Alison must have been sinking in as Kate now chatted on about her mother. She seemed to understand that we were following in her mother's footsteps to K2. She asked if her mother's mess tent would also have had windows in it. At the sight of all the porters carrying luggage and bringing tea, she commented that we must be very special to have such a welcome. I said, 'Well, it's because your mum was special.'

'Mum was special in climbing,' Kate added. Yes, I replied, she had climbed K2 and Everest. Then she said in a rather quaint adult way: 'Yes, Everest was a very happy thing, but it is terribly sad about K2 isn't it?' I agreed as Kate went on, 'I didn't want her to die'.

I tried to explain what had happened: 'None of us wanted her to die, and it's very sad that there was a big wind'.

'No, there was a storm, and it blew Mummy away,' corrected Kate. Her understanding was pleasing; she was obviously processing what she had heard.

Tom's school had assigned him the task of recording his journey in drawings and simple sentences, and as he tired from this classwork he responded well to the introduction of a book that Dr Dora Black had recommended for working through grief in children. The book, called *What to Do When Someone Very Special Dies: Children Can Learn to Cope with Grief*, is designed for children aged six to twelve years old and encourages them to express their feelings and perceptions in drawings, symbols and words.

I started this session with an open mind and with some anxiety. We sat on a towel, at the edge of the camp site. On a bank above us the local children had lined up and watched fascinated as Tom got caught up in his colourful drawings. He was so engrossed that he did not seem to notice the dozen children looking on for the full two hours, nor did he seem aware of the camera pointed at us from 4 metres away.

Tom worked hungrily through the book, often impatient to draw more and more. He listened intently as I read the comments on each page, trying to explain how things change through life. Change creates loss, and the pain from loss is called grief. Grief comes and goes, like the waves in the ocean; there will be stormy times and calm times. I explained how dead was the end of living. Without hesitation he did two drawings to represent living and dead – simply one figure upright and one horizontal. When asked to draw the ways people die, his first was guns and bullets, then stabbing, then drowning. He then did a careful drawing of his mother and only after he had finished it did he show how she died: the triangular mountain was dramatically outlined on the page, followed by fast and heavy strokes of black pencil representing the storm. He listened with interest and concentration at my explanation of death – that when someone dies, they can never come back, that the dead don't eat, drink, sleep, think or feel anything. I felt Tom was beginning to construct his own concepts of death and dissolving any fantasies about a reunion with his mother.

After this session I felt exhausted but Tom was happy and, after playing for a while in the stream, joined in with a game of cricket. In the evening he looked tired and troubled, threatening to work himself up into one of his tail-spin tempers. He left the mess tent where we had just finished eating and disappeared for half an hour into the darkness on his own. When he returned he told his dad that he had been thinking about Mum.

Two days later we had another session working through the book. Tom had asked to look at it. Kate joined us as we sat at the table in the mess tent and David helped her with some drawings. I worked with Tom and reviewed what he had done so far in his 'special book'. Kate listened in and watched with interest. Eventually she insisted on joining in and so I introduced her to a copy of the book. They both enjoyed discussing emotions and showed how to express feelings of happiness, sadness and guilt. Tom had been unaware of the camera filming us from 6 metres away but suddenly spotted them and realized they had been watching him for the last hour. Understandably, he felt betrayed, and lashed out in anger – an emotion he had been practising only moments before. He paced up and down to the camera, sticking his tongue out and shouting at the BBC not to film him. We all felt guilty. Chris Terrill explained they had not filmed any of his drawings but Tom was not impressed. We wondered if he would ever forgive us but I was pleased that this little boy felt able to express his anger so freely.

Kate spent over an hour doing a drawing of her mother. In the picture her dress got more and more elaborate, her face more and more covered in make-up and her jewellery ended up quite extensive. Kate's memory of her mother was of a very pretty, feminine woman who could look tremendous on a special occasion. This was certainly true but most people, including myself, would remember her as the fresh-faced, smiling, athletic strong climber. This aspect of her mother was certainly not the one that Kate felt was the most important.

The children took to the trekking without problems, apart from Tom's tummy upset one night and a grand total of two sticking plasters for Kate. At Paiju, David got dysentery and was really very unwell. Jim was very supportive and sensed my anxiety, not only as the doctor but as the wife of the casualty, and it helped that we were able to agree quickly on a plan from there. As it all worked out, I don't think we lost anything in terms of the children's emotional journey. We were able to have the 'au revoir' ceremony in view of K2 and, after all, that was the aim of the trip.

That day was difficult for Tom but he had been preparing himself for it and it became obvious when we got to the chosen site that he had a clear plan of what he wanted to do. He went to walk with his dad and Kate, and I couldn't help feeling proud of the way he was dealing with things. Tom set to work building his cairn and Kate copied from a few yards away. Jim sat and watched as the children built their memorial mounds of stones around the silk flowers and pictures they had chosen to leave. It just felt so right.

Afterwards, as the BBC interviewed Jim, Kate explained to me that 'Mummy had tried her best to come down and see us, but she just couldn't, the storm was so strong'. She said that when she left her last time, her mum had told her that she would return for Christmas. Now she wouldn't be there at Christmas but her spirit would come. Kate then helped me build my own cairn and built a representation of her mother with small stones, grass and flowers. 'Mummy will be able to see this for ever,' she said. She produced a piece of the remaining stalk from which her silk flower had been cut and decided that she would also leave this for Mum. But on looking at it again, grew doubtful – the bit of green stalk did look a bit dull. Then her face lit up. 'This stalk will grow into a flower just like the one in my cairn,' she said. 'Then Mummy will have three beautiful flowers to look at.' We finally turned back from this very special place. I could not imagine a more beautiful tribute to Alison.

ACKNOWLEDGMENTS: We would like to thank Dr Dora Black MB; FRCPsych, DPM, Director of the Traumatic Stress Clinic, 73 Charlotte Street, London, W1P 1LB; Jenny Kenrick at the Tavistock Clinic for support and advice and Dr Andrew Pollard of St Mary's Hospital, London W2 for advice on children at altitude. The Dean, Professor Lesley Rees and staff from Clinical Pharmacology, St Bartholomew's Hospital, for their forbearance. Mr Nigel Watson from the pharmacy at St Bartholomew's Hospital met our pharmaceutical needs at very short notice. Anthea Cridlan and Roger Courtiour from the BBC's Documentary Department for commitment beyond the call, and the film crew – Chris Terrill, Chris Openshaw, Adrian Bell and Andrew 'Andy Pandy' Thompson (Kate's favourite) for their discretion. Also my trainer, Dr Justin Livingston, and the staff and partners of the Elizabeth Avenue Group Practice in Islington, London, for their help and understanding.

The book used with Tom and Kate, *What to Do When Someone Very Special Dies: Children Can Learn to Cope with Grief* by Marge Heegaard is published by Woodland Press, Minneapolis, 1991 (available by mail order from Meditec, Medical and Nursing Booksellers, Jackson's Yard, Brewery Hill, Grantham, Lincs NG31 6DW, telephone 01476 590505).

FURTHER ACKNOWLEDGMENTS

Our adventure would have been impossible without the help and consideration of the following people.

Baltistan: the deputy commissioner, superintendent of police Hashmatullah Khan, the mayor of Skardu, the Crown Prince, and district council member Haji Eazil Ali.

BBC Books: Heather Holden-Brown, Frank Phillips, David Cottingham, Kate Lock, Khadija Manjlai and Alice Yglesias.

BBC Documentaries: Paul Hamann, Kaylene Arthurs, Adrian Bell, Anthea Cridlan, Roger Courtiour, Bhupinder Kohli, Olivia Lichtenstein, Chris Openshaw, Chris Terrill and Andrew Thompson.

British High Commission, Islamabad: Sir Roger and Lady MacRae, Tim Hitchens, Simon Minshull and Karen Rae.

Calanage Ltd, Stockport, Cheshire

Ferrino & C.S.p.A., San Mauro, Torino, Italy

Foreign and Commonwealth Office: Steve Ascombe, James Clark and Richard Morgan.

Laboratoires Garnier, London

Holas Hosiery, Baby, Leicester

The Lynx Agency, London

Marion Merrell Dow Ltd, Uxbridge, Middlesex

Nevis Range plc, Fort William, Lochaber

Nevisport Ltd, Fort William, Lochaber

Pakistan: President Farooq Ahmad Khan Leghari, Prime Minister Benazir Bhutto, Nazir Ahmad Alvi, Muzammil Pasha, Asem Mustafa Awan, Daniel Lak, Lionello Fogliano, Ashraf Aman, Dr David Beg, Joan Beg and Manzook Hussain.

Pakistan High Commission, London: Wajid Shamsul Hasan, Kamran Shafi, Massoud Khalid.

Pakistan International Airlines (London): Saleem Nisar, Kamran Ali Khan, Gaston du Chalus, Akram Janjua, Marion Lawrence and Hamid Ellam.

Pakistan International Airlines (Pakistan): Salman Javed, Muhammed Zaka Ullah Khan, Mirza Beg, Nishat Chishti, Zahir Hayat and Mamoon Shaikh.

Pakistan Ministry of Information: Anwar Mahmood, Akthar Hassan and Noor Saghir Khan.

Pakistan Tourism Development Corporation: Riaz Hussain Qureshi, Raja Changez Sultan, Syed Ishtiaq Hussain, Sher Ali, Abdul Rackman, Wahale.

Pelican Products Ltd, Salford, Manchester

Royal Navy and Royal Marines Mountaineering Club, Institute of Naval Medicine, Gosport, Hants

Sprayway Ltd, Manchester

Viking Optical Ltd, Halesworth, Suffolk

W. Jordan (Cereals) Ltd, Biggleswade, Bedfordshire

ScotRail, Glasgow

Wayfarer Outdoor Food, Malton, North Yorkshire

We would also like to thank Annette Allen, Steve Archibald, Marian Austin, Ian Baird, Keith Burne, Jo Cardwell, Tony Cardwell, Helen Cormack, Rita Coupland, David Donaldson, Xavier Eguskitza, David Evans, John Ferguson, Andrea Ferrino, Helen Gallon, Ian Gibson, David Govern, Simon Hawkes, Amanda Hill, Gavin Hogg, Alex Holland, Steve Holland, Bob Honey, Valerie Howland and the staff at Caol Nursery School, Alison Hood, John Hunt, Lieutenant Commander Steve Jackson, Philip Johnson, Bill Jordan, Nicola Lever, Jan Marshall, Nick Mason, Beth McGhie and the staff of Kilmonivaig Primary School, Dan McGrory, Virginia Mullen, Mark O'Shaughnessy, Bryony Ritchie, Geraldine Ritchie, Ronnie Robb, Iris Smith, Catherine Sutherland, Ian Sykes, Bill Wylie and Mickey Yule.

INDEX